W9-CMF-769

料理教室

CULINARY SKILLS LESSON

魚 鮮 • 蝦 甜 • 蟹 香
SEAFOOD INDULGENCE

序　Foreword

　　港人嗜吃海鮮，往往不惜花費金錢及時間，前往偏遠的海鮮熱點如西貢、流淨山或鯉魚門等地細味品嘗滋味海鮮，以滿口腹之欲。

　　市場上供應的海鮮品種五花八門，捧場客大不乏人，若有烹飪興致在家親自動手弄，當中的過程及成果，肯定令人雀躍不已！

　　因此，近月來我不斷構思及實踐不少海鮮菜式，現挑選40多款滋味海鮮與讀者分享，圖文並茂，解釋詳盡，希望讀者能在省錢大前題下，又能容易掌握烹調海鮮的方法，享受箇中的樂趣！

Hong Kong people love seafood. To indulge the appetite, they are willing to spend time and money to go to popular seafood places such as Sai Kung, Lau Fau Shan and Lei Yue Mun to pursue tasty seafood cuisines; no matter how far they are.

There are many varieties of seafood sold in the market and most of them got many fans. If you like cooking at home, you'll find that both the cooking process and result are exciting.

As a result, I continuously design and cook many seafood cuisines in the recent few months. Here more than 40 recipes are chosen to share with the readers together with pictures and full illustrations. I hope that you cannot only save money by cooking seafood at home but also handle the method of cooking seafood and enjoy the cooking process.

黃美鳳

Contents 目　　錄

活 魚鮮甜
SWEET LIVE FISH

味 鮮活蝦 FRESH PRAWNS

蟹 香誘惑 TEMPTING CRABS

馬介休蟹肉薯球 88
Deep-fried Potato Balls with
Bacalhau and Crabmeat

川醬辣蟹銀絲煲 90
Sichuan Spicy Crab and Vermicelli
in Clay Pot

椰皇蟹肉缽仔蛋 93
Steamed Eggs and Coconut Juice
with Crabmeat

鹽香豆瓣奄仔蟹 96
Stir-fried Small Green Crabs with
Spicy Soybean Sauce

貝 類海產
SHELLFISH AND SEAFOOD

香茅辣椒炒東風螺 98
Stir-fried Spiral Babylon with
Lemongrass and Chilies

XO 醬煎金蠔 100
Fried Golden Dried Oysters with XO Sauce

十穀米釀鮮魷筒 102
Baked Stuffed Squid with Ten-grain Rice

金不換蒸鮮帶子 105
Steamed Fresh Scallops with Basil Leaves

海膽蒸蛋白 108
Steamed Sea Urchin with Egg White

瑤柱汁燴鮮鮑 110
Braised Abalones with Dried Scallops Extract

金盞海鮮燴 112
Braised Seafood and Zucchini in Golden Cup

椰皇海鮮焗飯 115
Baked Seafood Rice in King Coconut

鮑汁金銀帶子 118
Fried Scallops with Abalone Sauce
and Dried Scallop Shreds

黑椒醬爆蟶子皇 120
Stir-fried King Razor Clams with
Black Pepper Sauce

金銀蒜蒸象拔蚌仔 122
Steamed Geoduck Clams with Garlic Duo

沙爹雜錦海鮮串燒 125
Baked Seafood Skewers with Satay Sauce

銀絲香芹花蛤鍋 128
Clams with Vermicelli and
Chinese Celery in Clay Pot

理論課：選購海鮮七大訣竅
Theory Class: 7 Tips of Choosing Seafood

香港市場售賣的海鮮，通常分為活海鮮、冰鮮海鮮及急凍海鮮。面對林林總總之魚穫海產，大部份人摸着腦子不懂選購，或任由魚販挑這選那，作為一名精明的「海鮮廚神」，當然要由懂得選購海鮮材料入手。

選購活魚時，有何注意之處？
相信自己的眼睛，挑選游弋及活動能力強、魚身帶光澤及表皮無破損的鮮魚。

如何挑選活蟹？
被繩子綑綁的活蟹，難以得知其活動能力之強弱，但可留意以下幾點：活蟹的眼睛精靈多動；口吐泡沫；蟹鉗及蟹爪完整無脫落。

如何確知活鮑魚是否新鮮？
鮮活鮑魚會吸附物體，見鮑魚互相黏附或吸附在玻璃上，輕按其肉立即收縮的，皆是新鮮活鮑魚，若無上述的反應，建議不應購買。

如何挑選冰鮮魚？
若購買原條冰鮮魚，如紅衫魚、馬頭或木棉魚等，必須察看以下特徵：魚鱗鮮明；魚鰓鮮紅；魚眼晶亮、不帶灰暗；魚肉有彈性。

切塊出售的冰鮮魚，有何選購秘訣？
鮫魚、魚仲（懵仔魚）或大石斑等冰鮮魚，魚販習慣切塊出售，除觀察魚皮是否鮮明外，最重要是觀察魚肉的切口是否保持微微漲起的狀況，勿選肉質內陷的魚塊，因新鮮魚肉具彈性。

購買冰鮮蝦有何注意要點？
1. 蝦頭及蝦殼緊連不脫落；2. 蝦頭不發黑；3. 蝦殼鮮明、無黑點。

如何選購急凍海鮮？
主要觀察其顏色之鮮明度，若發覺顏色暗啞，即代表急凍時間過長，別選購為妙！

Seafood sold in Hong Kong can generally be classified into live seafood, chilled seafood and frozen seafood.

Many people do not know how to choose seafood especially there are so many varieties or they just let the fishmongers to pick for them. To be a smart seafood chef, of course you need to know how to choose a kind of seafood ingredient.

What are the tips when choosing live fish?

Believe in your own eyes and pick those live fishes that swim quickly, active, has shiny gloss at the body and no damages at the skin.

How to pick live crabs?

It's hard to know if the crabs are active if they are bundled by strings but you can still pay attention to the following points: the eyes of live crabs are shiny and move often; they spit out bubbles; and their pincers and legs are intact but not come off.

How to know if live abalones are fresh?

Live and fresh abalones would stick to objects. If the abalones stick to each other or stick to the glass tank, press their meat lightly and those that contract at once are fresh abalones. Those that do not have the above response are not suggested to be bought.

How to choose chilled fishes?

To choose whole chilled fishes such as golden thread, tilefish or big-eyed fish, you must check the following characteristics: shiny scales; red gills; bright eyes but not dull eyes; and elastic flesh.

What are the tips of choosing chilled fishes that are cut and sold in parts?

Fishmongers usually cut large chilled fishes like mackerel, cobia and large grouper into parts. Besides observing if the skin of those fishes is shiny, the most important point is to note if the cutting edge of flesh still swells lightly. Do not buy those with shrink flesh since fresh fish flesh is elastic.

How to pick chilled prawns?

1. Choose those with heads and shells linking together but not fall off; 2. Discard those with black heads; 3. Choose those with shiny shells without black spots.

How to choose frozen seafood?

Mainly pick those with bright color only. Those with dull color means they have been frozen for too long and should not be chosen!

示範課：魚類處理及切法介紹
Demonstration Class: Method of Preparing and Cutting Fish

如何去鱗、去鰓？
How to scale and remove gills from fish?

購買鮮魚時，一般魚販會幫忙去鱗及去鰓，但不一定完全清理乾淨（尤其近尾部及魚鰭部位），回家後應自行清理。

1. 用刀在魚身表面逆向刮過，使魚鱗飛脱（特別留意尾部及近魚鰭位置），徹底刮去魚鱗。
2. 由鰓部起輕剁一刀至魚腹，清楚看見魚鰓及魚腸等內臟。
3. 用刀將魚鰓及內臟一併拉出，用牙刷擦洗乾淨。

Fishmongers usually help to scale and remove gills from fish when we bought fish. But they generally would not scale completely (especially the scales near the tail and fins) and hence we need to do it ourselves at home.

1. Scrape along the length of fish body in a reverse direction with a knife (especially the scales near the tail and fins) so that all scales fall off.
2. Slit from the bottom part of head to the abdomen of fish with a knife, the gill and entrails can be seen clearly.
3. Pull out the gill and entrails altogether with a knife and rub clean with a toothbrush.

如何切魚片？
How to slice fish?

1. 預備利刀，將魚柳鋪平砧板上（魚皮朝下）。
2. 用刀切每件約 1 厘米厚件。

1. Prepare a sharp knife and lay flat fish fillet on a chopping board (with the skin facing down).
2. Slice fish into pieces of about 1 cm thick.

如何切魚球？
How to make "curl-up" fish pieces?

1. 預備利刀，將魚柳鋪平砧板上（魚皮朝下）。
2. 用刀切每件約 3 厘米厚件，炒煮後魚皮收縮即成魚球。

1. Prepare a sharp knife and lay flat fish fillet on a chopping board (with the skin facing down).
2. Slice fish into pieces of about 3 cm thick. The fish skin would shrink after stir-fried, the fish pieces curled up and look like balls.

如何切魚米？
How to chop fish into dices?

將魚柳切成條狀，再切成均稱的粒狀（每粒約 1 厘米）。

Cut fish fillet into strips and then cut each strip into dices (of about 1 cm long in length) of equal sizes.

碧綠桂魚片

Stir-fried Mandarin Fish with Broccoli

COOKERY FORUM

1 斤重之桂花魚，可起出多少魚片？

How many fish slices can be obtained from 600 g of mandarin fish?

約可起出 6 兩淨肉。

About 225 g of fish flesh.

醃料內為何加入蛋白？

Why egg white is used as one of the marinade?

魚肉與蛋白拌勻，炒煮後魚肉可保持嫩滑的口感。

Fish mixed with egg white keeps smooth after stir-fried.

為何灒入薑汁酒？灒紹酒可以嗎？

Why ginger wine is used? Can it be replaced with Shaoxing wine?

薑汁酒可辟除魚腥味，適合炮製鮮魚菜式。

Ginger wine can remove fishy taste and is best for fish dishes.

炒桂花魚片時，魚肉容易鬆散嗎？

Would the mandarin fish slices scatter when stir-fried?

建議在炒煮魚片時，勿太大力拌炒，以免魚片散碎。

It is suggested to stir-fry the fish slices lightly to avoid them scattered.

材料 Ingredients

桂花魚 1 尾（約 1 斤重）
西蘭花 8 兩
甘筍 8 片
薑汁酒 1 湯匙
蒜茸 1 茶匙

1 mandarin fish (about 600 g)
300 g broccoli
8 slices carrot
1 tbsp ginger wine
1 tsp minced garlic

醃料 Marinade

鹽半茶匙
胡椒粉少許
蛋白 2 湯匙
生粉 1 茶匙

1/2 tsp salt
ground white pepper
2 tbsps egg white
1 tsp caltrop starch

調味料 Seasoning

水 3 湯匙
鹽半茶匙
糖 1/4 茶匙

3 tbsps water
1/2 tsp salt
1/4 tsp sugar

獻汁 Thickening sauce

水 3 湯匙
蠔油半湯匙
糖 1/4 茶匙
麻油少許
生粉半茶匙

3 tbsps water
1/2 tbsp oyster sauce
1/4 tsp sugar
sesame oil
1/2 tsp caltrop starch

準備工夫 Preparation

- 桂花魚起肉（魚販可代勞），切件，加入醃料拌勻醃 10 分鐘。
- 西蘭花修切成小棵，洗淨，放入滾水內飛水，盛起。
- Bone mandarin fish (or ask the fishmonger for help). Cut into slices and marinate for 10 minutes.
- Cut broccoli into florets. Rinse. Scald in boiling water and drain.

做法　Method

1. 熱鑊下油，放入西蘭花及調味料拌炒，盛起。
2. 燒熱油，爆香蒜茸，放入桂花魚片炒至熟，攢薑汁酒，下西蘭花、甘筍片及獻汁拌炒，滾後即可上碟。

1. Add oil into a hot wok. Put in the broccoli and seasoning. Stir-fry well and set aside.
2. Heat oil in wok. Stir-fry minced garlic until fragrant. Add the mandarin fish and stir-fry until done. Drizzle in ginger wine. Add broccoli, carrot slices and the thickening sauce. Mix well and cook until boiled. Serve.

蝦乾鮫魚餅

Fried Mackerel and Dried Shrimps Cakes

材料　Ingredients

鮫魚肉 8 兩
蝦乾半兩
韭菜粒 3 湯匙

300 g boned mackerel
19 g dried shrimps
3 tbsps diced Chinese chive

調味料　Seasoning

鹽半茶匙
魚露 2 茶匙
胡椒粉少許
浸泡蝦乾水 2 湯匙

1/2 tsp salt
2 tsps fish gravy
ground white pepper
2 tbsps water from
soaking dried shrimps

除用扁鮫魚肉外，還可用甚麼魚？
What other fish can be used except the flat mackerel?

可選用鯪魚或其他品種的鮫魚，但扁鮫魚的肉質及膠質最適宜，令魚餅更具彈性。
Dace or other kind of mackerel can be used. But the texture of flat mackerel is most suitable for fried fish cakes as it is elastic and chewy.

一尾鮫魚可刮出多少魚茸？
How much flesh can be obtained from a mackerel?

一尾約 1.5 斤重之鮫魚，可刮出約 1 斤魚茸。購買時可請魚販代起魚肉。
A mackerel weighed 900 g can give about 600 g of flesh. You can simply ask the fishmonger for boning.

加入浸泡蝦乾水有何作用？
What's the point of adding water from soaking dried shrimps?

泡浸後的清水帶蝦乾之鮮香味，別浪費，當調味料加入魚餅後，加倍提升魚餅的鮮味。
Don't waste the water from soaking dried shrimps as it has fresh shrimp taste. It can enhance the flavor of the fish cakes as the seasoning.

準備工夫 Preparation

- 鮫魚肉用匙羹依逆紋刮出魚肉。
- 蝦乾洗淨，浸軟，切粒（浸泡蝦乾水留用）。
- Scoop flesh from mackerel with a spoon along the vein in a reverse direction.
- Rinse dried shrimps. Soak until soft and dice (reserve the water from soaking dried shrimps.)

做法

1. 鮫魚茸、蝦乾、韭菜粒及調味料拌勻，順一方向攪拌至起膠，分成 15 等份，搓成魚餅。
2. 燒熱油，下魚餅用慢火煎至金黃色及熟透，上碟即成。

Method

1. Mix the mackerel flesh, dried shrimps, diced Chinese chive and seasoning. Stir in a direction until sticky. Divide into 15 portions and knead into fish cakes.
2. Heat oil in wok. Fry the fish cakes over low heat until golden brown and done. Serve.

酸 梅 椒 醬 蒸 魚 雲

Steamed Big-head Carp with Sour Plums and Chilies in Soybean Sauce

材料 Ingredients

大魚頭 12 兩
酸梅 3 粒
指天椒 3 隻
磨豉醬 2 茶匙
蒜茸 2 茶匙
薑絲 2 湯匙
葱粒 2 湯匙

450 g big-head carp
3 sour plums
3 bird's eye chilies
2 tsps ground soybean sauce
2 tsps minced garlic
2 tbsps shredded ginger
2 tbsps diced spring onion

調味料 Seasoning

鹽 1/4 茶匙
糖 1 湯匙
老抽 1 茶匙

1/4 tsp salt
1 tbsp sugar
1 tsp dark soy sauce

這款椒醬的味道有何獨特之處？

What's the unique flavor of this soybean sauce?

集甜、酸、辣於一身，配魚雲蒸煮，惹味好吃！

It's the combination of sweet, sour and spicy flavor. Steamed with fish head, this sauce is super tasty!

如何選購大魚頭？

How to choose big-head carp?

必須選購新鮮的大魚頭，否則帶魚腥味。

It is a must to choose fresh fish head or else it brings fishy smell.

通常買一瓶磨豉醬回來，很久也吃不完，怎辦？

How to handle the remaining bottle of ground soybean sauce?

可到雜貨店購買散裝的磨豉醬，隨每次用量購買，毋須囤積於雪櫃。

You can just buy the amount of ground soybean sauce you need each time at the grocery store, so that a whole bottle need not be stored in the refrigerator.

準備工夫 Preparation

- 大魚頭切成6至8件（魚販可代勞），洗淨，瀝乾水分。
- 酸梅去核，剁成茸。
- 指天椒去籽，切絲。
- Cut big-head carp into 6 to 8 pieces (or ask the fishmonger for help). Rinse and drain.
- Core and mince sour plums.
- Seed bird's eye chilies and shred.

做法 Method

1. 調味料、酸梅茸、指天椒、磨豉醬、蒜茸及薑絲拌勻。
2. 將上述之調味料與大魚頭拌勻，放入碟內，隔水蒸8分鐘，灑入蔥粒，再蒸半分鐘即成。

1. Mix the seasoning, minced sour plums, bird's eye chilies, ground soybean sauce, minced garlic and ginger shreds.
2. Mix the above seasoning with the fish head. Put into a plate and steam for 8 minutes. Sprinkle over spring onion dices and steam for 30 seconds more. Serve.

蕉葉烤魚
Baked Sole Fillet with Banana Leaf

哪裏購買蕉葉？若買不到，可用其他葉片代替嗎？

Where to buy banana leaf? If it cannot be found, can it be replaced with other leaves?

蕉葉於泰式雜貨店有售，價錢相宜，也可用糭葉或荷葉代替。

Banana leaf can be bought from Thai grocery stores and its price is reasonable. Or it can be replaced with wrapping leaves for rice dumplings or lotus leaves.

蕉葉必須拖水嗎？

Is it a must to scald banana leaf?

當然，令蕉葉軟身，容易包裹。

Of course. Scalding softens the leaf so that it is easy for wrapping.

材料　Ingredients

龍脷柳 2 件（約 8 兩）
乾葱茸 1 湯匙
蒜茸 1 湯匙
蕉葉 1 張
青檸 1 個

2 pieces sole fillet (300 g)
1 tbsp minced shallot
1 tbsp minced garlic
1 banana leaf
1 lime

醃料　Marinade

鹽半茶匙
胡椒粉半茶匙
魚露 2 茶匙
油 2 茶匙

1/2 tsp salt
1/2 tsp ground white pepper
2 tsps fish gravy
2 tsps oil

準備工夫 Preparation

- 龍脷柳解凍，洗淨，吸乾水分，加入醃料、乾葱茸及蒜茸醃 15 分鐘。
- 蕉葉裁剪成 30 厘米 x 30 厘米之正方形（共 2 張），洗淨，拖水，取出備用。
- 預熱焗爐 220℃；青檸切成角形。
- Defrost sole fillet. Rinse and wipe dry. Marinate together with minced shallot and minced garlic for 15 minutes.
- Trim banana leaf into 2 squares of sizes 30 cm by 30 cm. Rinse and scald. Set aside.
- Preheat oven to 220°C. Cut lime into wedges.

做法　Method

1. 魚柳放於蕉葉上（啞色面），摺入蕉葉，包成長方形，用牙籤固定兩端，包成兩份。

2. 將蕉葉魚包放入焗爐內，烤焗約 18 分鐘至熟透，取出，灑入青檸汁伴食。

1. Put sole fillet on top of the banana leaf (coarse side). Fold up into rectangular shaped and fix the ends with toothpicks. Make 2 sets altogether.

2. Bake the wrapped sole fillet in an oven for about 18 minutes until done. Sprinkle over lime juice and serve.

魚 腸 煎 蛋

Fried Eggs with Fish Intestines

如何處理魚腸？
How to handle the fish intestines?

整副魚腸包括魚腸、魚肝及魚脂，可保留魚肝與蛋液同煎，甘香美味；魚脂可棄掉。

The whole set of fish intestines include the intestines, the fish liver and also the fat. Keep the fish liver and fry it together with the eggs as it tastes fragrant while the fish fat can be removed.

如何徹底清洗魚腸？
How to rinse the fish intestines thoroughly?

灑入鹽於魚腸及魚肝，用手抓洗數次，用水沖淨，最後用少許白醋多洗一次，用水沖淨即可烹調。

Pour salt over the fish intestines and the fish liver, rinse with hand several times. Lastly add a little white vinegar and rinse once more. It is ready for cooking.

還有其他淡水魚腸可代替嗎？
Can I use intestines from other freshwater fishes?

鯇魚腸比其他淡水魚腸略大，而且煎後甘香味美。

The intestines from grass carp are larger and also taste good after frying.

為何魚腸先用薑米炒香？
Why are the fish intestines stir-fried with chopped ginger first?

薑味可辟除魚腸之腥味，潷酒，更可進一步去掉魚腥味。

Ginger removes the fishy smell from fish intestines and sizzling in wine also helps.

材料 Ingredients

鯇魚腸 2 副　　2 sets grass carp intestines
雞蛋 3 個　　　3 eggs
芫茜 1 棵　　　1 sprig coriander
葱 1 條　　　　1 sprig spring onion
薑 1 片　　　　1 slice ginger
紹酒半湯匙　　1/2 tbsp Shaoxing wine

調味料 Seasoning >1

生抽半湯匙
1/2 tbsp light soy sauce

調味料 Seasoning >2

生抽 1 茶匙
胡椒粉少許

1 tsp light soy sauce
ground white pepper

- 鯇魚腸用剪刀剪開，刮去污物，去掉肥膏，徹底洗淨，飛水，抹乾後切段，備用（有部份魚販可代處理魚腸，或需酌收費用）。
- 芫茜及葱切碎；薑切成幼粒。
- Trim open the grass carp intestines with a pair of scissors and scrape away any dirt. Remove the fat and rinse thoroughly. Scald and wipe dry. Cut into section and set aside (you may ask fishmonger to prepare fish intestine).
- Finely chop coriander and spring onion. Chop ginger into small dices.

做法 Method

1. 雞蛋拂勻，加入芫茜、葱及調味料（1）拂勻。

2. 燒熱油，下魚腸及薑米炒香，灒紹酒，加入調味料（2）拌炒，傾入蛋液煎成金黃香脆的蛋餅，趁熱享用。

1. Whisk eggs. Add in coriander, spring onion and seasoning (1). Mix well.

2. Heat oil in wok. Add the fish intestines and chopped ginger. Stir-fry until fragrant. Pour over Shaoxing wine lightly. Put in seasoning (2) and stir-fry well. Add the egg mixture and fry until crispy and golden brown. Serve hot.

乾 煎 香 蒜 三 文 魚 扒
Fried Salmon Steak with Garlic

三文魚有何益處？
What's the advantage of salmon?

三文魚含豐富的 Omega 3 不飽和脂肪酸，有助腦部發展及降低膽固醇，有益健康。
Salmon is rich in Omega 3-unsaturated fatty acid. It helps the development of the brain and reduces cholesterol thus good for health.

煎魚時毋須下大量油分嗎？
Why is it not necessary to add much oil for frying salmon?

由於三文魚扒含豐富的魚油，主要靠魚之油分煎熟即可。
Since salmon contains much fat, its fat can help to fry the fish until done.

準備工夫 Preparation
- 三文魚扒解凍，抹乾水分，用醃料抹勻醃 1 1/2 小時，盡量抹掉滲出的水分。
- 燒熱油，下蒜粒用中慢火炸成金蒜，備用。
- Defrost salmon steaks and wipe dry. Rub over the marinade and set aside for 1 1/2 hours. Remove away any water excreted from the fish.
- Heat the boil. Deep-fry the garlic over medium-low heat until golden. Set aside.

材料 Ingredients
三文魚扒 2 件（約 10 兩）
蒜粒 2 湯匙

2 salmon steaks (about 375 g)
2 tbsps chopped garlic

醃料 Marinade
鹽 2 茶匙

2 tsps salt

做法 Method
1. 平底鑊內燒熱油 2 茶匙，用小火將三文魚扒兩面煎至微黃及熟透，上碟。
2. 灑上金蒜，即可品嘗。

1. Heat 2 tsps of oil in a frying pan. Fry salmon steaks over low heat until both sides are golden brown and done.
2. Sprinkle over the deep-fried garlic and serve.

乾 煎 香 蒜 三 文 魚 扒

冬 瓜 金 腿 魚 夾
Steamed Wintermelon, Grouper and Jinhua Ham Sandwiches

斑肉及金華火腿如何釀得美觀？
How to stuff in grouper and Jinhua ham prettily?

斑肉及金腿的厚度必須切得較薄，高度比冬瓜件略短，釀入後更美觀。

The thickness of grouper slices and Jinhua ham slices should be thinner than that of wintermelon slices and their height should be a bit shorter than that of wintermelon.

這是 4 人份量嗎？
Is this dish for 4 persons?

是的，但斑肉、冬瓜及金腿的份量預備較多，以備不時之需。

Yes, but the amounts of grouper flesh, wintermelon and Jinhua ham are more for any sudden need.

應選購冬瓜的哪部份？
Which part of wintermelon should be chosen?

建議購買整個冬瓜的中間部份，瓜肉較軟身，容易釀入餡料。

Buy the middle part of wintermelon which is soft and easier for stuffing in fillings.

材料 Ingredients

石斑肉 3 兩
冬瓜 10 兩
金華火腿 1 兩
清雞湯 125 毫升

113 g grouper flesh
375 g wintermelon
38 g Jinhua ham
125 ml chicken broth

醃料 Marinade

鹽 1/8 茶匙
胡椒粉少許
蛋白 1 茶匙
生粉 1 茶匙

1/8 tsp salt
ground white pepper
1 tsp egg white
1 tsp caltrop starch

獻汁（拌勻）
Thickening sauce (mixed well)

清雞湯 100 毫升
糖 1/4 茶匙
麻油 1 茶匙
生粉 1 茶匙

100 ml chicken broth
1/4 tsp sugar
1 tsp sesame oil
1 tsp caltrop starch

準備工夫 Preparation

- 冬瓜去皮，切成約 5 x 4 x 2 厘米之厚件（共 12 件），在瓜肉直切兩刀（不切斷成雙飛狀）。
- 燒滾水，下油 1 茶匙及冬瓜件煮 3 分鐘，取出，待涼。
- 斑肉切成 12 件，加入醃料拌勻。
- 金華火腿切成 12 小片。
- Skin wintermelon and cut into thick slices of sizes about 5 x 4 x 2 cm (altogether 12 slices). Slit each slice at a side twice without cutting through.
- Bring water to the boil. Add 1 tsp of oil and cook the wintermelon for 3 minutes. Set aside to let cool.
- Cut grouper flesh into 12 pieces and mix with the marinade.
- Cut Jinhua ham into 12 small slices.

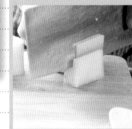

做法　Method

1. 將斑肉及金華火腿慢慢地釀入冬瓜內（或用小刀協助釀入），排在碟上，注入清雞湯蒸約 6 分鐘，隔去餘汁。
2. 煮滾獻汁，澆在冬瓜火腿魚夾上即可。

1. Stuff grouper slices and Jinhua ham into the wintermelon slices slowly (or use a small knife for help). Arrange them on a plate. Pour in chicken broth and steam for about 6 minutes. Pour away the extract.
2. Bring the thickening sauce to the boil and pour over the wintermelon. Serve.

Cookery Lesson 1 >4 至 5 人份量

咖喱三文魚頭粉皮煲

Simmered Salmon Head and Vermicelli Sheet with Curry Sauce in Clay Pot

材料 Ingredients

三文魚頭 1 個（約 1 斤 4 兩）
即食粉皮 1 包
咖喱醬 1 1/2 湯匙
咖喱粉 1 茶匙
乾葱頭 4 粒
椰漿半杯（125 毫升）
紅辣椒 1 隻（切圈，裝飾用）

1 salmon head (about 750 g)
1 pack instant vermicelli sheet
1 1/2 tbsps curry paste
1 tsp curry powder
4 shallots
1/2 cup (125 ml) coconut milk
1 red chili (cut into rings for garnishing)

COOKERY FORUM

粉皮毋須處理嗎？
Is it necessary to handle the vermicelli sheet ?

粉皮呈軟身，即開即煮，於大型凍肉食品店有售。
Vermicelli sheet is soft and is ready for cooking. It can be bought from large frozen food stores.

這道菜辣味濃郁嗎？
Is this dish spicy?

此菜屬於中級辣味，但卻滲有陣陣濃烈的咖喱香氣。
This dish belongs to medium spicy but it has strong curry fragrance.

用瓦鍋烹煮，有何注意之處？
What should be noted when cooking with clay pot ?

先用慢火令瓦鍋預熱，再調至中慢火炒香配料；上桌時建議用厚瓦碟墊着瓦鍋。
Preheat clay pot over low heat for a while then stir-fry the condiments over medium-low heat until fragrant. Also it is recommended to place thick clay dish below the clay pot on the dining table.

醃料 Marinade

鹽 1 茶匙

胡椒粉少許

薑汁酒 1 湯匙

生粉 1 1/2 湯匙（後下）

1 tsp salt

ground white pepper

1 tbsp ginger wine

1 1/2 tbsps caltrop starch
 (added at last)

調味料 Seasoning

水 1 1/2 杯

魚露 2 湯匙

胡椒粉少許

糖 1 茶匙

1 1/2 cups water

2 tbsps fish gravy

ground white pepper

1 tsp sugar

準備工夫 Preparation

- 三文魚頭洗淨，斬件，與醃料拌勻醃 15 分鐘。
- 粉皮隔去水分，備用。
- Rinse salmon head and chop into pieces. Marinate for 15 minutes.
- Drain vermicelli sheet and set aside.

做法 Method

1. 燒熱適量油，魚頭抹上生粉，放入油鍋內炸透，盛起。

2. 瓦鍋內燒熱少許油，下乾葱頭、咖喱醬及咖喱粉爆香，加入魚頭及調味料煮滾，燜煮約 10 分鐘，最後下粉皮及椰漿煮滾，裝飾後上桌品嘗。

1. Heat oil in a wok. Coat the salmon head with caltrop starch and deep-fry until done. Drain.

2. Heat a little oil in a clay pot. Stir-fry shallots, curry paste and curry powder until fragrant. Put in the fish head and seasoning. Bring to the boil and then simmer for about 10 minutes. Add vermicelli sheet and coconut milk. Bring to the boil. Garnish and serve.

鮮 菌 石 斑 球
Braised Grouper with Fresh Mushrooms

材料 Ingredients

石斑肉 8 兩 — 300 g grouper flesh
秀珍菇 3 兩 — 113 g oyster mushrooms
蟹味菇 2 兩 — 75 g beech mushrooms
西芹 2 兩 — 75 g celery
甘筍 8 片 — 8 slices carrot
薑數片 — several slices ginger
蒜茸 1 茶匙 — 1 tsp minced garlic
乾葱茸 1 茶匙 — 1 tsp minced shallot
紹酒 2 茶匙 — 2 tsps Shaoxing wine

醃料 Marinade

鹽 1/3 茶匙
胡椒粉少許
蛋白 1 湯匙
生粉半湯匙

1/3 tsp salt
ground white pepper
1 tbsp egg white
1/2 tbsp caltrop starch

調味料 Seasoning

鹽 1/3 茶匙
水適量

1/3 tsp salt
water

COOKERY FORUM

炒斑肉有何竅門？
What's the tip of stir-frying grouper flesh?

炒魚球必須輕力拌炒，否則魚肉容易鬆散。
Grouper flesh must be stir-fried lightly or otherwise it will break into pieces.

如何去除鮮菇的異味？
How to remove unfavorable smell from fresh mushrooms?

烹調前緊記先飛水，可去掉鮮菇的異味。
Scald mushrooms before cooking can remove their unfavorable smell.

如何去掉西芹的老筋？
How to remove hard strings from celery?

可撕去老筋或用小刀刨去西芹表面的老筋。
Just tease them off or peel its skin with a small knife.

獻汁（拌勻）
Thickening sauce (mixed well)

水 4 湯匙	4 tbsps water
鹽 1/4 茶匙	1/4 tsp salt
蠔油半湯匙	1/2 tbsp oyster sauce
糖 1/4 茶匙	1/4 tsp sugar
麻油及胡椒粉各少許	sesame oil
生粉 1 茶匙	ground white pepper
	1 tsp caltrop starch

準備工夫 Preparation

- 斑肉切件，加入醃料拌勻醃 10 分鐘。
- 秀珍菇及蟹味菇切去根部，洗淨備用。
- 西芹切成斜段。
- Cut grouper flesh into pieces and marinate for 10 minutes.
- Cut off roots from oyster mushrooms and beech mushrooms. Rinse and set aside.
- Section celery at an angle.

做法 Method

1. 秀珍菇及蟹味菇飛水，盛起，瀝乾水分。
2. 燒熱少許油，下西芹及調味料炒熟，盛起。
3. 斑肉泡油，盛起。
4. 熱鑊下油，下薑片、蒜茸及乾葱茸爆香，加入全部材料拌炒，灒紹酒，注入獻汁煮滾，拌勻上碟。

1. Scald oyster mushrooms and beech mushrooms. Drain.
2. Heat a little oil in a wok. Add celery and seasoning. Stir-fry until done and set aside.
3. Scald grouper flesh in oil for a while and drain.
4. Add oil into a hot wok. Stir-fry ginger slices, minced garlic and minced shallot until fragrant. Put in all ingredients. Pour in Shaoxing wine and the thickening sauce. Bring to the boil. Mix well and serve.

黃 金 芙 蓉 魚 米

Stir-fried Fish Dices with Corn Kernels and Egg Whites

應選擇哪款魚柳切成魚米？
Which kind of fish fillet should be chosen to make fish dices?

魚柳可選用斑肉、青衣肉或龍脷柳等。
Grouper, green wrasse or sole fillet can be used.

用甚麼火候炒蛋白魚米？
What level of heat should be used to stir-fry the fish dices?

炒魚米時用中慢火，令蛋白魚米呈雪白色澤，又不焦燶。
Stir-fry fish dices over medium-low heat can give the egg white and fish dices snow white gloss and also not charred.

如何有效地剝出完整之粟米粒？
How to tear out whole corn kernels effectively?

先剝掉一直行之粟米粒，其餘的就能輕易及完整地剝出。
Tear away a line of corn kernels then the remaining can be easily torn out in whole.

可用罐裝粟米粒代替嗎？
Can it be replaced with canned corn kernels?

當然可以，但清甜味當然不及新鮮粟米粒。緊記粟米粒必須徹底吸乾水分，才與蛋白同炒，否則菜式會滲出水分，影響味道。
Of course, but their taste is not as fresh and sweet as that of fresh corn kernels. Remember to wipe dry the corn kernels thoroughly before stir-frying with egg whites or else the dish becomes watery.

材料 Ingredients

魚柳 4 兩
新鮮粟米粒 3 湯匙
蛋白 5 個
芫茜 1 棵

150 g fish fillet
3 tbsps fresh corn kernels
5 egg whites
1 stalk coriander

醃料 Marinade

鹽及雞粉各 1/4 茶匙
胡椒粉少許
生粉半茶匙
油 1 茶匙

1/4 tsp salt
1/4 tsp chicken powder
ground white pepper
1/2 tsp caltrop starch
1 tsp oil

調味料 Seasoning

清雞湯 1/3 杯
鹽 1/4 茶匙
糖 1/8 茶匙
麻油及胡椒粉各少許
生粉半湯匙

1/3 cup chicken broth
1/4 tsp salt
1/8 tsp sugar
sesame oil
ground white pepper
1/2 tbsp caltrop starch

準備工夫 Preparation

- 魚柳洗淨，抹乾水分，切粒，加入醃料醃 5 分鐘。
- 芫茜切碎。
- 粟米粒用滾水煮約 2 分鐘至熟透，盛起待涼。
- Rinse fish fillet and wipe dry. Dice and marinate for 5 minutes.
- Chop coriander.
- Cook corn kernels in boiling water for about 2 minutes until done. Set aside to let cool.

做法 Method

1. 熱鑊下油，下魚米炒至半熟，盛起，待涼。
2. 蛋白拂勻，加入調味料、魚米及芫茜拌勻。
3. 熱鑊下油，注入蛋白混合物及粟米粒炒至剛凝固，上碟，趁熱享用。

1. Add oil into a hot wok. Stir-fry fish dices until medium cooked. Set aside to let cool.
2. Whisk egg whites. Mix in the seasoning, fish dices and coriander.
3. Add oil into a hot wok. Pour in the egg white mixture and corn kernels. Stir-fry until just set. Serve hot.

頭 抽 煎 焗 大 鱔

Fried Eel with Premium Soy Sauce

材料 Ingredients

白鱔 12 兩
陳皮 1/8 個
蒜茸 2 湯匙
葱粒 1 1/2 湯匙

450 g white eel
1/8 dried tangerine peel
2 tbsps minced garlic
1 1/2 tbsps diced spring onion

醃料 Marinade

鹽 2/3 茶匙
胡椒粉少許
生粉半湯匙（後下）

2/3 tsp salt
ground white pepper
1/2 tbsp caltrop starch (added at last)

調味料（拌勻）
Seasoning (mixed well)

水 1 湯匙
頭抽 2 湯匙
糖 1 茶匙

1 tbsp water
2 tbsps premium soy sauce
1 tsp sugar

用易潔鑊煎白鱔有何好處？
What are the benefits of frying eel with non-stick pan?

由於白鱔油分多，可省卻用油量，而且減低白鱔之油膩感。
Since white eel is rich in oil, it can save a lot of oil and also reduce the greasiness of the eel.

為何在鱔皮上切成 V 型？
Why slit V shapes at the eel skin?

使鱔皮斷開，煎時不會太蜷曲，賣相更佳。
It breaks open the skin so that it would not curl up during frying and it appears good presentation.

可用普通生抽代替頭抽嗎？
Can premium soy sauce replaces by normal light soy sauce?

可以，但味道卻比頭抽略遜。
Yes, but the flavor reduces.

- 白鱔去掉潺液，切成半吋厚鱔件（魚販可代勞），洗淨，抹乾，在鱔皮上往肉處切成 V 型，下醃料醃 10 分鐘（煎前才拌入生粉）。
- 陳皮用水浸軟，刮去瓤，切絲。
- Remove slime from white eel and cut into 1/2 inch thick slices (or ask the fishmonger for help). Rinse and wipe dry. Slit V shapes at the skin and marinate for 10 minutes (add caltrop starch right before frying).
- Soak dried tangerine peel until soft. Scrape off the pith and cut into shreds.

做法 Method

STEP BY STEP

1. 易潔鑊下少許油，加入鱔件煎至微黃色，反轉再煎，加入陳皮絲及蒜茸，加蓋焗片刻。
2. 灒入調味料，煮至汁液乾透，最後灑入葱粒，上碟品嘗。

1. Heat a little oil in a non-stick frying pan. Fry the eel slices until slightly golden. Turn upside down and fry. Put in shredded dried tangerine peel and minced garlic. Cover the lid and cook for a while.
2. Pour in the seasoning. Cook until the sauce is dry. Add diced spring onion and serve.

自 製 甜 椒 醬 伴 鮫 魚
Fried Mackerel with Sweet Pepper Sauce

材料 Ingredients

鮫魚 4 件（約 8 兩）
甜青椒 4 兩
甜紅椒 4 兩
紫洋葱 1 1/2 兩
清水 150 毫升

4 pieces mackerel (about 300 g)
150 g green bell pepper
150 g red bell pepper
57 g purple onion
150 ml water

醃料 Marinade

鹽半茶匙
胡椒粉少許
生粉 1 湯匙（後下）

1/2 tsp salt
ground white pepper
1 tbsp caltrop starch
(added at last)

調味料 Seasoning

茄汁 1 1/2 湯匙
是拉差辣椒醬半湯匙
鹽 1/3 茶匙
糖 1 湯匙

1 1/2 tbsps ketchup
1/2 tbsp Sriracha chili
sauce
1/3 tsp salt
1 tbsp sugar

除鮫魚外，還可選擇哪種魚？
What fish can be used except mackerel?

銀鱈魚及三文魚也是不錯之選擇，而且營養價值非常高。

White cod fish and salmon are good choices as they are high in nutritional value.

步驟似乎很繁複，容易掌握嗎？
Would it be easy to handle these rather complicated steps?

其實步驟並不複雜，只要將青紅甜椒及洋蔥分成 3/4 份及 1/4 份，前者製成椒茸；後者作為配料即可。

In fact the steps are not complex. Just divide green and red bell peppers as well as the purple onion into 3/4 portion and 1/4 portion; and the former is used to make minced pepper while the latter is used as condiments.

甚麼是「是拉差辣椒醬」？
What is Sriracha chili sauce?

這是一款泰式辣椒醬，辣味濃重，於泰式雜貨店有售。

This is a kind of Thai chili sauce which has strong spicy flavor and can be bought from Thai grocery stores.

準備工夫 Preparation

- 鮫魚洗淨，抹乾水分，與醃料拌勻醃 10 分鐘。
- 青紅甜椒及紫洋蔥各 1/4 份量切絲，其餘切粒。
- Rinse mackerel and wipe dry. Marinate for 10 minutes.
- Shred 1/4 portion of green bell pepper, red bell pepper and purple onion. Dice the remaining portions.

做法　Method

1. 燒熱適量油，下青紅椒絲及洋蔥絲炒透，盛起。
2. 下青紅椒粒及洋蔥粒炒透，放入攪拌機內，傾入 1/3 份量清水打成甜椒茸，備用。
3. 魚塊均勻地灑上生粉，下熱油內煎熟，上碟。
4. 煮滾甜椒茸、調味料及餘下之清水，加入青紅椒絲及洋蔥絲拌勻，澆在魚塊上享用。

1. Heat oil in a wok. Add shredded green and red bell peppers and purple onion shreds. Stir-fry well and set aside.
2. Stir-fry diced green and red bell peppers and diced purple onion thoroughly. Put into a blender and add 1/3 portion of water. Blend into minced pepper.
3. Coat fish evenly with caltrop starch. Fry in hot oil until done. Put on a plate.
4. Bring the minced pepper, seasoning and the remaining water to the boil. Mix in the green and red bell peppers shreds as well as the purple onion shreds. Pour the sauce over the fish and serve.

鰻魚汁煎銀鯧
Fried Pomfret with Eel Sauce

如何令鯧魚更入味？
How to make the pomfret more flavorful?

鯧魚洗淨後必須徹底抹乾，塗上醃料才容易入味。

Wipe dry the pomfret thoroughly after rinsed so that the flavor of the marinade gets into the fish easily.

鰻魚汁不宜太早放入？
Why eel sauce is not added at the early stage?

對，太早放入容易令魚焦燶。

It makes the fish charred easily if added too early.

如何確知魚身熟透？
How to know if the fish is done?

當見魚肉由軟身轉為結實；骨和肉略為分離，即表示魚身熟透。

When the fish flesh turns from soft to hard and when the bones and flesh are a bit separated then the fish is done.

準備工夫 Preparation

- 鯧魚去腸，洗淨，抹乾，下醃料塗勻魚身，醃 2 小時。
- 調味料拌勻。
- Remove the intestine from pomfret. Rinse and wipe dry. Rub marinade over the whole fish and set aside for 2 hours.
- Mix well the seasoning.

材料　Ingredients

鯧魚 1 尾（約 12 兩）
鰻魚汁 2 湯匙
薑絲 1 湯匙
葱白 1 湯匙
紹酒 1 湯匙

1 pomfret (about 450 g)
2 tbsps eel sauce
1 tbsp shredded ginger
1 tbsp white part of spring onion
1 tbsp Shaoxing wine

醃料　Marinade

鹽 3/4 茶匙
胡椒粉少許

3/4 tsp salt
ground white pepper

調味料　Seasoning

水 3 湯匙
糖 1/3 茶匙

3 tbsps water
1/3 tsp sugar

做法 Method

1. 燒熱油，下薑絲及葱白爆香，放入鯧魚煎透兩面，讚紹酒。

2. 灑入鰻魚汁及調味料煮至汁液濃稠，上碟享用。

1. Heat oil in wok. Stir-fry shredded ginger and white part of spring onion until fragrant. Add pomfret and fry both sides thoroughly. Sizzle in Shaoxing wine.

2. Pour in eel sauce and the seasoning. Cook until the sauce thickens and serve.

海 皇 蝦 湯 脆 米

Seafood and Rice in Prawn Broth with Crispy Rice

COOKERY FORUM

如何自製鮮蟹肉？
How to make crabmeat on my own?

購買花蟹或肉蟹（約重 12 兩），隔水蒸 14 分鐘，待涼，可拆出 3 至 4 兩蟹肉。

Buy coral crab or mud crab (about 450 g) and steam for 14 minutes. Set aside to let cool and bone to take 113 g to 150 g of crabmeat.

如何煮成半生熟米飯？
How to cook medium-cooked rice?

白飯煲至中途時，見飯水成蝦眼狀（微滾），取出米飯，即成半生熟米飯，可炸成鬆脆的米粒。

Take up the rice when it is lightly boiled or the bubbles are in prawn-eye shaped. This rice can be deep-fried into crispy rice grains.

烹調蝦湯有何竅門？
What are the tips of cooking prawn broth?

必須煎香蝦頭及蝦殼，再用慢火熬煮至濃郁的蝦湯，令湯味特別鮮香美味！

The prawn heads and prawn shells must be fried until fragrant first. Then cook them over low heat until the broth thickens.

材料　Ingredients

斑肉 3 兩
中蝦 8 隻
鮮蟹肉 2 兩
白飯 1 1/2 碗
半生熟米飯 3 湯匙
西芹粒 2 湯匙
蝦湯 625 毫升

113 g grouper flesh
8 medium-sized prawns
75 g fresh crabmeat
1 1/2 bowls cooked rice
3 tbsps medium-cooked rice
2 tbsps diced celery
625 ml prawn broth

蝦湯材料
Ingredients of prawn broth

大蝦頭、蝦殼共 12 兩
滾水 1 公升
香葉 3 片
白胡椒粒半茶匙

450 g big prawn heads and shells
1 liter boiling water
3 bay leaves
1/2 tsp white peppercorns

醃料　Marinade

鹽 1/4 茶匙
胡椒粉少許
生粉半茶匙

1/4 tsp salt
ground white pepper
1/2 tsp caltrop starch

調味料　Seasoning

鹽半茶匙

1/2 tsp salt

準備工夫 Preparation

- 蝦頭及蝦殼洗淨，瀝乾水分。燒熱油，下蝦頭及蝦殼煎香，注入滾水、香葉及胡椒粒，用慢火煮 1 小時，至蝦湯濃縮至 625 毫升，下鹽調味。
- 斑肉洗淨，抹乾水分，切件；中蝦去殼、去腸，洗淨，用醃料拌勻醃 10 分鐘。
- 煲煮白飯期間，取出米飯成半生熟米飯，瀝乾水分。
- Rinse prawn heads and prawn shells. Drain. Heat oil in a wok and fry them until fragrant. Pour in boiling water, bay leaves and peppercorns. Cook over low heat for 1 hour until 625 ml of prawn broth remained. Season with salt.
- Rinse grouper flesh and wipe dry. Cut into pieces. Shell and devein prawns. Rinse and marinate for 10 minutes.
- Take up the rice when cooking to give medium-cooked rice and drain.

做法 Method

1. 熱鑊下油，加入蝦球及魚肉炒熟，盛起。
2. 燒熱油，下半生熟米飯炸脆，瀝乾油分。
3. 西芹粒用滾水灼熟，盛起。
4. 鍋內放入白飯，下斑肉、蝦球、蟹肉及西芹粒，注入熱蝦湯，最後灑上脆米，伴湯享用。

1. Add oil into a hot wok. Put in shelled prawns and grouper flesh. Stir-fry until done and set aside.
2. Heat oil in wok. Deep-fry medium-cooked rice until crispy and drain.
3. Blanch diced celery in boiling water until done and drain.
4. Put cooked rice into a pot. Add grouper flesh, prawns, crabmeat and diced celery. Pour in hot prawn broth. Lastly sprinkle over the deep-fried rice and serve with the broth.

小 白 菜 魚 餃 湯 鍋

Fish Dumplings and Small White Cabbages in Fish Broth

魚餃材料
Ingredients of fish dumplings

鮫魚肉 1 片（約 5 兩），臘腸半條，芫茜 1 棵，葱 1 條，圓型水餃皮 10 張

1 piece mackerel flesh (about 175 g),1/2 preserved sausage, 1 stalk coriander, 1 sprig spring onion, 10 round dumpling wrappers

魚湯材料
Ingredients of fish broth

鮮魚 1 斤，薑 2 片，滾水 1.25 公升

600 g fresh fish, 2 slices ginger, 1.25 liters boiling water

配料 Condiment

小白菜 4 兩

150 g small white cabbages

調味料 Seasoning >1

鹽 1/4 茶匙，胡椒粉少許，水及生粉各 2 茶匙

1/4 tsp salt, ground white pepper, 2 tsps water, 2 tsps caltrop starch

調味料 Seasoning >2

鹽適量

salt

準備工夫（魚餃） Preparation of fish dumplings

- 鮫魚肉用匙羹順逆紋刮出魚肉。
- 臘腸隔水蒸 10 分鐘，待涼，切細粒。
- 芫茜及葱切粒。
- 魚茸、臘腸、芫茜、葱及調味料（1）放於大碗內，順一方向攪拌成魚餃餡料，分成 10 份。
- 將餡料放入水餃皮內，用水輕抹皮邊，摺成呈窩型的魚餃。
- Scoop flesh from mackerel with a spoon along the vein in a reverse direction.
- Steam preserved sausage for 10 minutes and set aside to let cool. Cut into small dices.
- Chop coriander and spring onion.
- Put fish flesh, preserved sausage, coriander, spring onion and seasoning (1) into a large bowl. Stir in one direction to become the filling and divide into 10 portions.
- Put the filling on top of the wrappers. Dip water at the sides and wrap into nest-shaped fish dumplings.

STEP BY STEP

COOKERY FORUM

哪種魚可打成魚茸？
Which kind of fish can make paste?

鹹水魚檔有售之鮫魚、狗棍；淡水魚檔之鯪魚皆可。

Mackerel and lizard fish bought from saltwater fish stalls or dace bought from freshwater fish stalls can do.

包摺魚餃有何竅門？
What are the tips of wrapping fish dumplings?

1. 釀入適量之餡料；2. 平均地捏摺魚餃；3. 封口時穩固，必定能成功包成魚餃。

Firstly, stuff in suitable amount of fillings; secondly, knead the fish dumplings evenly; and thirdly, binding the ends well can help you make fish dumplings successfully.

通常用哪款鮮魚熬湯？
What kind of fresh fish is usually used to make fish broth?

牛鰍魚、梭羅魚、三文魚骨、狗棍及木棉魚皆可熬成魚湯，鮮甜美味！

Flathead fish, solo fish, salmon bones, lizard fish or big-eyed fish can be cooked into tasty fish broth.

準備工夫（魚湯）
Preparation of fish broth

- 燒熱油，下鮮魚及薑片煎香，放入魚袋內，注入滾水煮約 1 小時，至餘下 2 1/2 杯（625 毫升）魚湯，下鹽調味。
- Heat oil in wok. Fry fish and ginger slices until fragrant. Put the fish into a cloth bag and cook in boiling water for about 1 hour until 2 1/2 cups (625 ml) of fish broth remained. Season with salt.

做法 Method

1. 煮滾一鍋水，下魚餃煮熟及浮起，盛起。
2. 取出魚湯內之魚袋，放入小白菜煮熟，下魚餃煮滾即可享用。

1. Bring a pot of water to the boil. Add the fish dumplings. Cook until done and floats up. Drain.
2. Remove the cloth bag from the fish broth. Add small white cabbages and cook until done. Put in fish dumplings and bring to the boil. Serve.

示範課：鮮蝦處理及打蝦膠

Demonstration Class: Method of Preparing Fresh Prawn and Prawn Paste

從街市買回新鮮活蝦，建議先將蝦冷藏 2 小時，冷凍後容易去掉外殼。

It is recommended to refrigerate live prawns for 2 hours before cooking so that their shells are easy to be removed.

如何去掉蝦頭及蝦殼？
How to remove the heads and shells from prawns?

1. 將蝦頭用手扭脫，與蝦身分離（見圖 1 及 2）。
2. 慢慢剝掉蝦殼，蝦尾緩緩退出，保留完整的蝦肉（見圖 3 及 4）。
3. 可保留蝦頭及蝦殼，熬煮成蝦湯。

1. Twist off heads from prawns with hand (as shown in 1-2).
2. Tear off shell from prawns slowly and push out the tail slowly. The intact prawn flesh can be kept (as shown in 3-4).
3. Can cook prawn heads and shells into soup.

❶

❷

3

4

蝦肉剔背及去腸有何技巧？
What are the steps of deveining prawns?

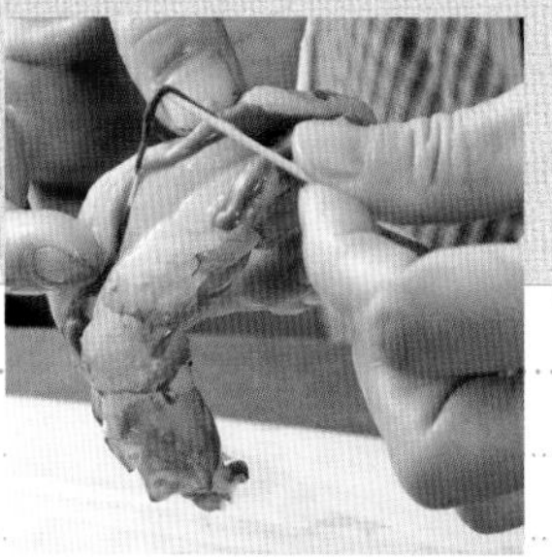

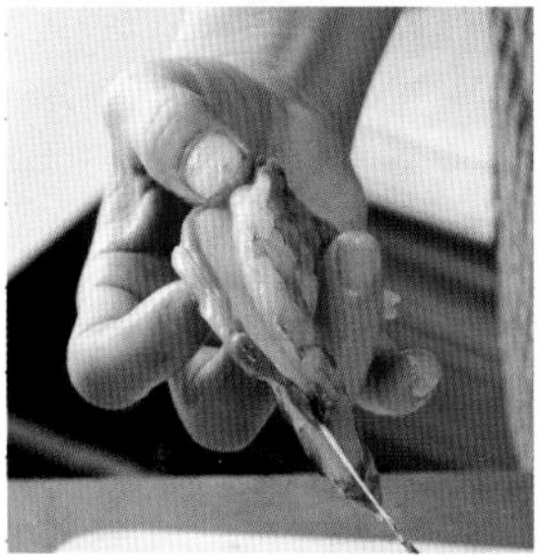

1. 將蝦肉鋪平在砧板上，沿背部輕剔一刀。
2. 用牙籤於背部挑去蝦腸，用鹽及生粉抓洗，再用水沖淨。

1. Lay flat shelled prawns on a chopping board and slit lightly along the back of prawns.
2. Devein at the back with a toothpick. Rub prawns with salt and caltrop starch. Rinse with water.

如何切蝦球？
How to make "curl-up" prawns?

選購活中蝦、大蝦或優質冰鮮蝦，沿背部位置輕剔一刀，去腸，炒煮後蝦肉收縮即成蝦球。

Choose live medium-sized prawns, large prawns or premium chilled prawns. Slit lightly along the length at the back of prawns without cutting through. Devein. The prawns curl up after stir-fried.

自製蝦膠有何訣竅？
What are the tips of making prawn paste?

想成功炮製蝦膠，打蝦膠時，碗內必須徹底乾淨，緊記不可沾有蒜、薑等食材，否則難以打成蝦膠。

1. 蝦肉處理後放於砧板上，用刀面大力拍扁蝦肉，再用刀面推壓開來（見圖 1 至 3）。

2. 用刀背在蝦肉上略剁成蝦茸（見圖 4 及 5）。

3. 放入深碗內，順一方向攪拌至起膠即成，冷藏 1 小時後使用，效果更佳。

The bowl for making prawn paste must be thoroughly clean and should not have any other ingredients like garlic and ginger. Otherwise, prawn paste cannot be made successfully.

1. Put prawn flesh on a chopping board and pat prawn with the flat side of a knife forcefully. Press flat to a side with the flat side of a knife (as shown in 1-3).

2. Chop prawn with the back of a knife briefly into mashed prawn (as shown in 4-5).

3. Put mashed prawn into a deep bowl. Stir in one direction until sticky. For better effect, refrigerate the prawn paste for 1 hour before cooking.

烹飪小疑問

購買一斤連殼的活蝦回來，可得多少淨蝦肉？
How much prawn flesh can be obtained from live prawns with shells weighing 600 g?

帶殼的蝦隻，去掉蝦頭及蝦殼等，約可得原重量一半之淨蝦肉，即一斤活蝦約可得半斤蝦肉。

Prawn flesh weighing about half of original weight of prawns can be obtained after removing heads and shells from prawns. Thus about 300 g of prawn flesh can be got from 600 g of prawns.

示範課：龍蝦處理方法
Demonstration Class: Preparing Lobster

如何劏龍蝦及起肉？
How to gut and shell lobsters?

1. 於龍蝦尾部插入筷子，流出尿液（見圖 1）。
2. 彎起龍蝦身，於龍蝦頭及身之間的空隙用刀切下，分開龍蝦頭及蝦身（見圖 2 及 3）。
3. 剪開蝦腹兩邊的薄膜，去掉薄膜，小心地取出完整之龍蝦肉（見圖 4 至 7）。

1. Insert a chopstick into the lobster at its tail to let out urine from the lobster (as shown in 1).
2. Curl up the lobster body. Cut where the head joins the body with a knife (as shown in 2-3).
3. Cut open the thin membrane at the abdomen of lobster with a pair of scissors and remove the membrane. Take out the flesh in intact carefully (as shown in 4-7).

①

2

3

④

⑤

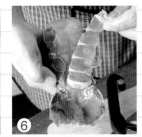
6

7

椒鹽金蒜瀨尿蝦
Mantis Prawns with Spiced Salt, Chilies and Garlic

材料 Ingredients

瀨尿蝦 2 隻（約 1 斤）　2 mantis prawns (about 600 g)
粗粒蒜茸 3 湯匙　3 tbsps coarsely diced garlic
紅辣椒 1 隻　1 red chili
指天椒 2 隻　2 bird's eye chilies
紹酒半湯匙　1/2 tbsp Shaoxing wine
淮鹽 1 茶匙　1 tsp spiced salt
冰水適量　iced water

淮鹽材料
Ingredients of spiced salt

幼鹽 1 湯匙
五香粉 3/4 茶匙

1 tbsp table salt
3/4 tsp five-spice powder

COOKERY FORUM

瀨尿蝦灼煮後，為何用冰水泡浸？
Why soak mantis prawns in iced water after blanched?

令瀨尿蝦的肉質爽脆，而且容易脫殼。
This makes their texture crunchy and their shells easy to be removed.

家人不嗜辣，怎辦？
What can I do if my family member does not prefer spicy taste?

去掉紅辣椒及指天椒即可，味道依然美味！
Just get rid of red chili and bird's eye chilies. The dish still tastes good.

用小瀨尿蝦炒煮，食味相同嗎？
Would small mantis prawns give same taste?

食味略有差別，因小瀨尿蝦的肉質及鮮味比大瀨尿蝦略遜。
There's a little difference in taste since the texture and freshness of small mantis prawns are not as good as large ones.

準備工夫 Preparation

- 燒熱油，下粗粒蒜茸炸至金黃色成金蒜。
- 紅辣椒及指天椒去籽、切絲。
- 白鑊炒熱幼鹽，關火，加入五香粉拌成淮鹽，備用。
- Heat oil in wok. Deep-fry diced garlic until golden brown.
- Seed red chili and bird's eye chilies. Cut them into shreds.
- Stir-fry table salt in a wok without oil until hot. Remove heat and mix in five-spice powder to become spiced salt. Set aside.

做法 Method

1. 煮滾一鍋水，放入已洗淨之瀨尿蝦灼煮4分鐘，取出，浸泡於冰水至凍，切件，吸乾水分。
2. 燒熱適量油，下瀨尿蝦炸透，盛起。
3. 熱鑊下油1湯匙，加入紅辣椒及指天椒爆香，下瀨尿蝦拌炒，灒紹酒，灑入淮鹽及金蒜，拌勻上碟即可。

1. Bring a pot of water to the boil. Blanch rinsed mantis prawns for 4 minutes. Drain and soak in iced water until cold. Cut into pieces and wipe dry.
2. Heat oil in wok and deep-fry mantis prawns thoroughly. Drain.
3. Add 1 tbsp of oil into a hot wok. Stir-fry red chili and bird's eye chilies quickly until fragrant. Put in mantis prawns and stir fry well. Pour in Shaoxing wine lightly. Sprinkle over spiced salt and deep-fried garlic. Mix well and serve.

蝦子頭抽煎海蝦

Shallow-fried Prawns with Premium Soy Sauce and Shrimp Roes

COOKERY FORUM

如何提升海蝦之鮮味？
How to enhance the taste of sea prawns?

海蝦配搭蝦子及頭抽炮製，有效提升蝦之鮮味。
Cooking sea prawns with shrimp roes and premium soy sauce can enhance the sweet taste.

何謂「半煎炸」？
What's mean by shallow-fry?

半煎炸的用油量比香煎的用油量略多，以半煎半炸之方式炮製，令蝦肉更爽口彈牙。
Using more oil than simply frying, the prawn has a crunchy texture.

哪裏購買即食蝦子？
Where to buy instant shrimp roes?

一般雜貨店或製麵條的店舖均有出售。
They can be bought from grocery stores or shops selling noodles.

準備工夫 Preparation

- 修剪蝦鬚及蝦腳；剪開蝦背，去腸，洗淨，吸乾水分。
- Trim prawn tentacles and legs. Cut open prawns at the back. Devein, rinse and wipe dry.

材料 Ingredients
海中蝦 8 隻（約 8 兩）
即食蝦子 2 茶匙
薑 2 片
葱絲適量

8 medium-sized sea prawns (about 300 g)
2 tsps instant shrimp roes
2 slices ginger
spring onion shreds

調味料 Seasoning
頭抽 1 1/2 湯匙
糖 2 茶匙
水 1 湯匙

1 1/2 tbsps premium soy sauce
2 tsps sugar
1 tbsp water

做法 Method

1. 熱鑊下油，加入薑片爆香，下中蝦半煎炸至半熟，盛起，去掉薑片。

2. 煮滾調味料，中蝦回鑊，加蓋，煮至汁液乾透，灑入蝦子拌勻，上碟，以葱絲伴碟即可品嘗。

1. Add oil into a hot wok. Add ginger slices and stir-fry until fragrant. Put in medium prawns and shallow-fry until medium cooked. Set aside and remove the ginger slices.

2. Bring seasoning to the boil. Transfer medium prawns back to the wok and cover the lid. Cook until the sauce is just dry. Sizzle in shrimp roes and mix well. Garnish with spring onion shreds and serve.

Cookery Lesson 2
蝦 子 頭 抽 煎 海 蝦

一 蝦 兩 吃

Deep-fried Prawns with Wasabi Sauce and Kumquat Syrup

材料 Ingredients
大蝦 8 隻

8 large prawns

醃料 Marinade
鹽 1/8 茶匙
胡椒粉少許

1/8 tsp salt
ground white pepper

炸漿料 Deep-frying batter
蛋黃 2 個
水 1 湯匙
炸粉 2 湯匙

2 egg yolks
1 tbsp water
2 tbsps deep-frying powder

日式芥辣汁 Wasabi sauce
日式芥辣 1 湯匙
蜜糖 4 茶匙
水 4 湯匙
鹽 1/8 茶匙

1 tbsp wasabi
4 tsps honey
4 tbsps water
1/8 tsp salt

柑桔蜜汁 Kumquat syrup
蜜餞柑桔 3 粒（去核、剁碎）
檸檬汁半湯匙
糖 2 茶匙
水 3 湯匙

3 sweetened kumquat
 (cored and chopped)
1/2 tbsp lemon juice
2 tsps sugar
3 tbsps water

如何炮製鮮甜爽口的蝦？
How to cook sweet and crunchy prawns?

建議選購新鮮活蝦，鮮甜爽口，美味無窮！
Choose fresh and live prawns that taste sweet and crunchy.

甚麼是蜜餞柑桔？
What is sweetened kumquat?

涼果店有售之蜜餞柑桔，味道甜膩。
It is sold at dried fruits stores and tastes super sweet.

準備工夫 Preparation

- 大蝦去殼，開背、去腸，切成蝦球，洗淨，抹乾，加入醃料醃 15 分鐘。
- 蛋黃拂勻，拌入其餘炸漿料，備用。
- Shell large prawns. Cut open at the back and devein. Rinse and wipe dry. Marinate for 15 minutes.
- Whisk egg yolks and mix in the remaining ingredients of deep-frying batter. Set aside.

做法 Method

1. 大蝦蘸上炸漿，放入熱油內炸至金黃色及熟透，分成兩份，排於碟上。
2. 分別煮熱日式芥辣汁及柑桔蜜汁，伴大蝦享用即可。

1. Coat large prawns with the deep-frying batter. Deep-fry in hot oil until golden brown and done. Divide into 2 portions and arrange on a plate.
2. Heat the wasabi sauce and kumquat syrup respectively. Serve with the large prawns.

香 醋 荔 枝 百 花 球
Braised Stuffed Lychees with Prawn Paste in Zhenjiang Vinegar

可用罐裝荔枝代替嗎？

Can lychees replaced by canned ones?

此菜適宜用新鮮荔枝烹調，因罐裝荔枝的味道太甜了！

Fresh lychees are more suitable for this dish since canned lychees are too sweet.

蝦膠可預早一晚預備嗎？

Can I prepare prawn paste a day in advance?

絕對可以，能減輕烹煮當天的工作量。

Absolutely.

釀入的蝦膠容易脫落嗎？

Would prawn paste separate from lychees easily?

餡料不容易脫落，因去核的荔枝肉帶深窩，餡料能黏在荔枝肉內。

No, the fillings would not fall off easily since cored lychees have deep holes and the fillings can stick in the lychee flesh.

材料　Ingredients

蝦肉 3 兩
荔枝 12 粒
士多啤梨 5 個
蒜茸 1 茶匙

113 g shelled prawns
12 lychees
5 strawberries
1 tsp minced garlic

調味料　Seasoning

鹽 1/8 茶匙
胡椒粉少許
蛋白 1 茶匙

1/8 tsp salt
ground white pepper
1 tsp egg white

獻汁（拌勻）
Thickening sauce (mixed well)

鎮江醋 4 茶匙
糖 2 茶匙
水 3 湯匙
鹽 1/4 茶匙
生粉 1 茶匙

4 tsps Zhenjiang vinegar
2 tsps sugar
3 tbsps water
1/4 tsp salt
1 tsp caltrop starch

準備工夫 Preparation

- 蝦肉去腸，洗淨，抹乾水分，用刀拍成蝦膠，用刀背略剁，加入調味料順一方向拌至起膠，冷藏 1 小時備用。
- 士多啤梨洗淨，用冷開水略沖，切成兩份。
- 荔枝去皮、去核。
- Devein shelled prawns. Rinse and wipe dry. Pat prawns with the flat side of a knife and chop briefly with the back of a knife. Mix in seasoning and stir in one direction until sticky to become the prawn paste. Refrigerate for 1 hour and set aside.
- Rinse strawberries. Rinse with cold drinking water briefly and cut into halves.
- Peel and core lychees.

做法 Method

1. 取適量蝦膠釀入荔枝內，隔水蒸 5 分鐘，取出，隔去汁液。
2. 燒熱油，下蒜茸爆香，傾入獻汁煮滾，放入荔枝百花球及士多啤梨拌勻上碟。

1. Stuff prawn paste into lychees. Steam for 5 minutes and remove the extract.
2. Heat oil in wok. Stir-fry minced garlic quickly until fragrant. Pour in thickening sauce and bring to the boil. Add lychees and strawberries. Mix well and serve.

胡 椒 蝦
Fried Prawns with White Peppercorns

材料 Ingredients

中蝦 12 兩
白胡椒粒 1 1/2 至 2 湯匙
紅辣椒 2 隻
淮鹽 1 茶匙
清水 3 湯匙

450 g medium-sized prawns
1 1/2 to 2 tbsps white peppercorns
2 red chilies
1 tsp spiced salt
3 tbsps water

淮鹽料
Ingredients of spiced salt

幼鹽 1 湯匙
五香粉半茶匙

1 tbsp table salt
1/2 tsp five-spice powder

如何令蝦殼香脆美味？

How to make the prawn shells crispy and tasty?

改用炸的方法，下中蝦略炸至蝦殼香脆，但耗油量比煎的方法略多。

Use deep-frying rather than frying can make prawn shells crispy but it uses more oil.

如何令白胡椒粒的香氣滲入蝦內？

How to bring the smell of white peppercorns into the prawns?

白胡椒粒炒香後，放入蝦加蓋焗煮，令胡椒香氣滲入蝦肉。

Stir-fry white peppercorns until fragrant and then put in prawns. Cover the lid and cook for a while to bring the smell of white peppercorns into the prawns.

準備工夫 Preparation

- 白鑊炒熱幼鹽，關火，加入五香粉炒勻，盛起備用。
- 修剪蝦鬚及蝦腳，挑去蝦腸，洗淨，抹乾水分，用淮鹽醃 1 小時。
- 白胡椒粒略椿碎；紅辣椒切圈。
- Stir-fry table salt until hot in a wok without oil. Remove heat and mix in five-spice powder. Stir-fry well to become the spiced salt. Set aside.
- Trim prawn tentacles and legs. Devein, rinse and wipe dry. Marinate with spiced salt for 1 hour.
- Crush white peppercorns briefly. Cut red chilies into rings.

做法 Method

1. 熱鑊下油，放入中蝦略煎兩面，盛起。
2. 燒熱油，下白胡椒粒炒香，加入中蝦、紅辣椒及清水拌炒，加蓋焗煮片刻至汁液收乾，上碟，以羅勒裝飾享用。

1. Add oil into a hot wok. Fry both sides of medium prawns briefly. Set aside.
2. Heat oil in wok. Stir-fry white peppercorns until fragrant. Put in medium prawns, red chilies and water. Stir-fry well. Cover the lid and cook for a while until the sauce is dry. Garnish with basil and serve.

咕嚕百花釀油條
Shallow-fried Stuffed Dough Stick with Prawn Paste

材料 Ingredients

蝦肉 4 兩
油條 1 孖
西芹粒 2 湯匙

150 g shelled prawns
1 pair deep-fried dough stick
2 tbsps diced celery

醃料 Marinade

鹽 1/8 茶匙
胡椒粉少許

1/8 tsp salt
ground white pepper

蘸汁 Dipping sauce

水 4 湯匙，白醋 2 茶匙，糖 1 湯匙，茄汁 1 湯匙，生粉半茶匙

4 tbsps water, 2 tsps white vinegar, 1 tbsp sugar, 1 tbsp ketchup, 1/2 tsp caltrop starch

百花釀油條可預先釀妥嗎？

Can I stuff the prawn paste in advance?

絕對可以，百花釀油條釀妥後冷藏，享用時才炸脆，簡單方便。

Yes, you can stuff the prawn paste into the dough stick in advance and store in the refrigerator. Only fry it when going to serve. It is simple and convenient.

如何確知蝦肉餡料熟透？

How to know if the prawn fillings are done?

見蝦肉轉成紅色及肉質結實，即代表蝦肉熟透。

When the prawn flesh turns red colour and becomes firm in texture, it is done.

打蝦膠有何注意之處？

What should be noted about when stirring the prawn paste?

剁碎及拌蝦膠用之器皿必須徹底乾淨；拌蝦膠時順一方向用力攪拌，一定成功打出蝦膠。

The tools for chopping shelled prawns and the container for mixing prawn paste should be clean. Also stir in one direction in force can give prawn paste successfully.

準備工夫 Preparation

- 油條撕成兩條，剪成約 2 厘米之長度，備用。
- 蝦肉去腸，洗淨，抹乾水分，用刀拍打成蝦膠，加入醃料及西芹粒順一方向攪拌至帶黏性。
- Tease the dough stick into two pieces and cut into sections of about 2 cm long. Set aside.
- Devein shelled prawns. Rinse and wipe dry. Pat with the flat side of a knife to become the prawn paste. Add marinade and diced celery. Stir in one direction until sticky.

做法 Method

1. 將油條的軟麵糰部分掏出，釀入適量蝦膠。
2. 燒熱適量油，下百花油條半煎炸至餡熟皮脆，盛起。
3. 煮滾蘸汁，伴百花油條享用。

1. Scrape out the soft part from dough stick and stuff in the prawn paste.
2. Heat oil in a wok. Shallow-fry the stuffed dough stick until the fillings are done and the skin is crispy. Drain.
3. Bring the dipping sauce to the boil. Serve with the stuffed dough stick.

帶 子 百 花 石 榴 粿
Steamed Scallops and Prawns Beggar's Purses

蛋白皮材料
Ingredients of egg white wrappers

蛋白 8 個
生粉 2 茶匙
清水 2 湯匙

8 egg whites
2 tsps caltrop starch
2 tbsps water

蛋白皮調味料
Seasoning of egg white wrappers

鹽 1/3 茶匙

1/3 tsp salt

COOKERY FORUM

蛋白皮煎後，可放置一會才包裹餡料嗎？
Can egg white wrappers set aside for a while before wrapping?

建議蛋白皮煎後即包入餡料，否則蛋白皮皺摺，影響外觀。

It is recommended to wrap in fillings right after frying egg white wrappers, or they wrinkle and affect the appearance.

韭菜花容易折斷，怎辦？
How to do with the easy-broken flowering chives?

韭菜花先飛水才作包紮用途，只要小心處理，絕無問題，同時可多預備韭菜花作不時之需。

Scald flowering chives beforehand and handle carefully. Or you may also prepare more chives.

煎蛋白皮有何竅門？
What are the tips of frying egg white wrappers?

1. 火候細；2. 油分少；3. 蛋白漿塗勻平底鑊。

1.Fry over low heat; 2.use little oil only; 3. lay the egg white paste evenly in the frying pan.

蛋白皮料內為何加入生粉？
Why add caltrop starch into the egg white wrappers ingredients?

增加蛋白皮的韌度，包摺時不容易弄破。

It increases the hardness of egg white wrappers so they do not break easily during wrapping.

石榴粿餡料
Fillings of beggar's purses

帶子 4 隻
蝦肉 3 兩（去腸）
去皮馬蹄 2 粒
西芹 1 兩

4 scallops
113 g shelled prawns (deveined)
2 peeled water chestnuts
38 g celery

餡料調味料
Seasoning of fillings

鹽 1/3 茶匙
胡椒粉少許
麻油 1 茶匙

1/3 tsp salt
ground white pepper
1 tsp sesame oil

配料 Condiment

韭菜花 8 條
8 flowering chives

獻汁 Thickening sauce

清雞湯 6 湯匙
麻油少許
生粉 1 茶匙

6 tbsps chicken broth
sesame oil
1 tsp caltrop starch

準備工夫 Preparation

- 蛋白皮材料拌勻，加入調味料拌勻。平底鑊燒熱油，下蛋白料煎成薄薄蛋白皮（共8張），待涼備用。
- 帶子、蝦肉、馬蹄及西芹切粒。熱鑊下油，下餡料拌炒，加入調味料炒熟，分成8份，待涼。
- 韭菜花放入滾水內飛水至軟身，備用。
- Mix the ingredients of egg white wrappers. Add seasoning and mix well. Heat oil in a frying pan. Fry 8 thin egg white wrappers and set aside to let cool.
- Dice scallops, shelled prawns, water chestnuts and celery. Add oil into a hot wok. Put in the fillings and stir-fry well. Add seasoning and stir-fry until done. Divide into 8 portions and set aside to let cool.
- Scald flowering chives in boiling water until soft and set aside.

做法 Method

1. 蛋白皮鋪平，放入適量餡料包摺成石榴粿，用韭菜花包紮，放於碟上，隔水蒸5分鐘，取出。
2. 煮滾獻汁，澆在石榴粿上即可享用。

1. Lay flat the egg white wrappers and put in the fillings. Wrap the beggar's purses and fix the ends with chives. Put on a plate and steam for 5 minutes.
2. Bring the thickening sauce to the boil and pour over the beggar's purses. Serve.

芝 士 南 瓜 汁 龍 蝦 球

Lobster Chunks with Cheese and Pumpkin Sauce

材料 Ingredients

龍蝦 1 隻（約 1 斤重）
中國南瓜 4 兩
芝士片 2 塊

1 lobster (about 600 g)
150 g Chinese pumpkin
2 slices cheese

醃料 Marinade

鹽 1/4 茶匙
麻油及胡椒粉各少許
蛋白 1 湯匙
生粉 2 茶匙

1/4 tsp salt
sesame oil
ground white pepper
1 tbsp egg white
2 tsps caltrop starch

調味料 Seasoning

鹽 1/8 茶匙
水 4 湯匙

1/8 tsp salt
4 tbsps water

1 斤重之龍蝦，約可得多少龍蝦肉？
How much flesh can be obtained from 600 g of lobster?

切去龍蝦頭後，約可取得 5 兩淨肉。
About 188 g of flesh can be usually obtained from a lobster weighing 600 g after cutting the head.

在家不想用大量油泡油，怎辦？
What can be done if I do not want to use large amount of oil for cooking lobster?

龍蝦肉不泡油，烹調效果並不理想。若想省卻用油量，建議龍蝦肉分兩次泡油，可減省油量。
The effect is not good if lobster is not blanched in oil. To save the amount of oil used, you may cook lobster by two times.

可選用日本南瓜煮汁嗎？
Can Japanese pumpkin be used to cook the sauce?

日本南瓜的瓜肉較糯，配搭芝士烹調，口感膩滯，故建議選用中國南瓜。
Japanese pumpkin gives sticky mash and it tastes greasy if matched with cheese. Hence Chinese pumpkin is recommended.

準備工夫 Preparation

- 處理龍蝦及起肉之方法，參考第 53 頁。
- 蝦肉去腸，略沖，切件，用醃料拌勻醃 10 分鐘。
- 南瓜去皮，切件，隔水蒸 10 分鐘，壓成南瓜茸，備用。
- Refer to P.53 for preparing and shelling lobster.
- Remove entrails from lobster and rinse briefly. Cut into pieces and marinate for 10 minutes.
- Skin pumpkin and cut into pieces. Steam for 10 minute and press into puree. Set aside.

做法 Method

1. 燒熱適量油，下龍蝦球泡油至熟，上碟。
2. 燒熱少許油，下南瓜茸、芝士片及調味料煮滾，至芝士片溶化，澆在龍蝦球上，趁熱品嘗。

1. Heat oil in wok. Blanch the lobster in warm oil until done. Put on a plate.
2. Heat a little oil in a wok. Add pumpkin puree, cheese slices and seasoning. Bring to the boil until the cheese melted. Pour the sauce over the lobster and serve.

惹味蝦

Braised Prawns with Sweet, Sour and Spicy Sauce

材料 Ingredients

中蝦 8 兩

薑米 1 湯匙

葱 2 條

紹酒 1 湯匙

300 g medium-sized prawns

1 tbsp chopped ginger

2 sprigs spring onion

1 tbsp Shaoxing wine

調味料 Seasoning

水及鎮江醋各 1 1/2 湯匙

糖 1 湯匙

辣椒油半湯匙

鹽 1/4 茶匙

麻油 1 茶匙

1 1/2 tbsps water

1 1/2 tbsps Zhenjiang vinegar

1 tbsp sugar

1/2 tbsp chili oil

1/4 tsp salt

1 tsp sesame oil

蝦肉會煮至過熟嗎？
Would prawns be over-cooked?

中蝦煎至半熟（剛轉成紅色），注入調味料同煮，蝦肉不會煮得過熟。

Fry medium prawns until medium cooked (just turn red colour). Pour in the seasoning and cook it together with the prawns hence the prawns would not be over-cooked.

這款蝦的味道如何？
What's the taste of these prawns?

蝦肉滲滿甜、酸、辣、香之味，故稱為「惹味蝦」。

These prawns taste sweet, sour, spicy and fragrant.

若想方便進食，烹調前可先剝掉蝦殼嗎？
Can the prawns be shelled before cooking for easy consumption?

絕對可以，但調味需略調校，因蝦隻去掉外殼，味道會直接滲入蝦肉。

Absolutely, but the seasoning need to be adjusted. Since the prawns have been shelled, any taste would go into the prawns directly.

準備工夫 Preparation

- 修剪中蝦的蝦鬚及蝦腳，挑去蝦腸，洗淨，抹乾水分。
- 葱分成葱白及葱段。
- Trim prawn tentacles and legs. Devein, rinse and wipe dry.
- Cut spring onion into white parts and cut the green parts into section.

做法 Method

1. 熱鑊下油，加入薑米及葱白爆香，放入中蝦煎至剛轉成紅色，灒紹酒，傾入調味料，加蓋焗片刻。

2. 焗煮至調味料濃稠，最後灑入葱段拌炒，上碟。

1. Add oil into a hot wok. Put in chopped ginger and white part of spring onion. Stir-fry quickly until fragrant. Add medium prawns and fry until they just turn red colour. Sizzle in Shaoxing wine. Pour in seasoning and cover the lid.

2. Cook for a while until the seasoning thickens. Sprinkle over spring onion sections and stir-fry well. Serve.

示範課：劏蟹、拆蟹肉、拆蟹膏
Demonstration Class: Method of Gutting Crabs, Picking out Crabmeat and Crab Roe

購買活蟹回來，若非即時烹煮，可將活蟹（連繩）放於碟上，用濕布蓋着，可養活直至烹調（約一天）。

If live crabs are not going to be cooked after bought, put them (with string) into a plate and cover with a damp cloth. The crabs can live for about 1 day.

劏活蟹的步驟如何？
How to gut live crabs?

1. 將一雙筷子插入眼下的蟹蓋與蟹身之間的位置，待一會（見圖1）。
2. 筷子向前後拉開，容易分開蟹蓋及蟹身（見圖2及3）。
3. 去掉蟹鰓、內臟、胃部及腹部蟹奄（見圖4），清洗擦淨。
4. 用刀在蟹鉗的關節位斬開，分開蟹鉗及蟹身（見圖5）。
5. 將蟹身斬成兩份，每份再斬件兩小件（見圖6及7），隨時烹調。

1. Insert a pair of chopsticks into the crab below its eyes at the gap between the shell and its body. Set aside for a while (as shown in 1).
2. Pull open the shell by separating the chopsticks one to front and one to back (as shown in 2-3).
3. Remove the gill, entrails and stomach part (as shown in 4). Rinse and rub clean.
4. Cut the joint of the pincers from the crab body (as shown in 5).
5. Cut the crab body into two pieces and then each piece cut into two small pieces (as shown in 6-7).

如何拆鮮蟹肉？
How to get crabmeat?

蟹肉是常用的材料，自製鮮蟹肉，鮮甜味美，而且方便快捷，動手吧！

1. 蟹身及蟹鉗隔水蒸熟，待涼或冷藏 2 小時，容易拆出蟹肉。
2. 用刀略拍蟹鉗，拆出完整的蟹鉗肉（見圖 1 及 2）。
3. 用剪刀剪出蟹身白殼，用匙羹容易刮出蟹肉（見圖 3 至 5）。

＊注意：蟹肉內的碎殼必須徹底撿出。

Crabmeat is a common ingredient. Self-made fresh crabmeat tastes sweet and is also easy and convenient to make. Let's do it now!

1. Steam crab body and crab pincers until done. Set aside to let cool and refrigerate for 2 hours.
2. Pat the pincers briefly with a knife. Shell and get intact pincers' meat (as shown in 1-2).
3. Cut the white shell from crab body with a pair of scissors. Scrape out crabmeat with a spoon (as shown in 3-5).

＊ Attention: Any shell fragments in the crabmeat must be picked up completely.

如何拆蟹膏？
How to get crab roe?

蒸蟹前，於蟹蓋、蟹身上刮出蟹膏，待烹調前用滾水浸熟。

Scrape up crab roe from the shell and body of crab before steaming. Soak it in boiling water until done right before cooking.

椰 香 咖 喱 蟹
Curry Crab with Coconut Milk

如何保持濃郁的椰香味？
How to keep the rich coconut smell?

↓

最後傾入椰漿，勿煮太久，上桌時椰香四溢。
Pour in the coconut milk at the last and do not cook for too long, there is still rich coconut smell when serving.

咖喱醬為何用小火炒煮？
Why stir-frying curry sauce over low heat?

↓

令咖喱香氣慢慢散發出來，而且避免咖喱醬焦燶，影響食味。
This makes the curry fragrance emit out slowly and also avoids it get charred.

準備工夫 Preparation

- 肉蟹洗淨，斬件，瀝乾水分。
- 咖喱醬與水 1 湯匙拌勻。
- 紅辣椒、乾蔥及蒜頭切碎，備用。
- Rinse mud crab. Chop up into pieces and drain.
- Mix curry sauce with 1 tbsp of water.
- Chop red chili, shallot and garlic. Set aside.

材料 Ingredients

肉蟹 1 隻（約 1 斤重）
咖喱醬 1 1/2 湯匙
椰漿 125 毫升
紅辣椒 1 隻
乾蔥 1 粒
蒜頭 2 粒
薑 2 片

1 mud crab (about 600 g)
1 1/2 tbsps curry sauce
125 ml coconut milk
1 red chili
1 shallot
2 cloves garlic
2 slices ginger

調味料 Seasoning

清雞湯 125 毫升
鹽 1/3 茶匙
魚露 1 湯匙
糖 1/4 茶匙
胡椒粉少許
清水 60 毫升

125 ml chicken broth
1/3 tsp salt
1 tbsp fish gravy
1/4 tsp sugar
ground white pepper
60 ml water

做法 Method

1. 燒熱適量油，下蟹件炒至轉成紅色，盛起。
2. 熱鑊下油，下辣椒、乾蔥、蒜頭及薑片爆香，放入咖喱醬用小火爆香，放入蟹件及調味料拌勻，加蓋煮 10 分鐘。
3. 最後拌入椰漿煮滾，上碟即成。

1. Heat oil in a wok. Stir-fry crab until turns red colour. Drain.
2. Add oil into a hot wok. Stir-fry chili, shallot, garlic and ginger slices until fragrant. Put in curry sauce and stir-fry quickly over low heat until fragrant. Put in the crab and seasoning. Mix well and cover the lid. Cook for about 10 minutes.
3. Lastly pour in coconut milk and bring to the boil. Serve.

蟹肉桂花翅

Scrambled Eggs with Shark's Fin and Mung Bean Sprouts

可用急凍蟹肉代替嗎？

Can fresh crabmeat be replaced with frozen crabmeat?

絕對不可，因為鮮蟹肉是這道菜式之神髓，老饕可品嘗鮮甜之蟹肉香味。

No, because the essence of this dish lies in fresh crabmeat that tastes fresh and sweet.

炒蛋液時，最後為何澆入凍開水？

Why putting in cold drinking water at last when stir-frying the egg mixture?

灑入凍開水，令桂花翅不太乾及質感太粗。

Cold drinking water wets the shark's fin and egg mixture, it would not taste dry and rough in texture.

炒桂花翅的火候如何控制？

How to control the heat when stir-frying the shark's fin and egg mixture?

先用中火炒蛋液及蟹肉等材料，再調至小火炒至乾身，耐心處理必能成功。

Stir-fry the egg and crabmeat mixture over medium heat first and then turn to low heat and cook until dry. Patience can give you success.

材料 Ingredients

急凍魚翅 5 兩，鮮蟹肉 2 兩，銀芽 2 兩，雞蛋 5 個，紹酒 1 茶匙，凍開水 1 湯匙
188 g frozen shark's fin, 75 g fresh crabmeat, 75 g mung bean sprouts, 5 eggs,1 tsp Shaoxing wine, 1 tbsp cold drinking water

煨魚翅料
Ingredients for cooking shark's fin

薑 2 片，葱 3 條，紹酒 1 茶匙，清水 750 毫升，油 1 湯匙
2 slices ginger, 3 sprigs spring onion, 1 tsp Shaoxing wine, 750 ml water, 1 tbsp oil

調味料 Seasoning >1

鹽 1/4 茶匙
1/4 tsp salt

調味料 Seasoning >2

鹽 3/4 茶匙，麻油及胡椒粉各少許，粟粉 3/4 湯匙，油 1 湯匙，紹酒半湯匙
3/4 tsp salt,sesame oil, ground white pepper, 3/4 tbsp corn starch, 1 tbsp oil, 1/2 tbsp Shaoxing wine

準備工夫 Preparation

- 魚翅解凍，拆絲。
- 煮滾適量清水，放入魚翅煮至腍，盛起，瀝乾水分。
- 熱鑊下油，加入薑及葱爆香，灒紹酒，下清水、油1湯匙及魚翅煮5分鐘，盛起。
- Defrost shark's fin. Break it into shreds by hands.
- Bring water to the boil. Add shark's fin and cook until soft. Drain.
- Add oil into a hot wok. Stir-fry ginger and spring onion until fragrant. Pour in Shaoxing wine lightly. Add water, 1 tbsp of oil and shark's fin. Cook for 5 minutes and set aside.

做法　Method

1. 熱鑊下油，加入銀芽炒透，下調味料（1）炒勻，盛起，隔去水分。
2. 雞蛋及調味料（2）拂勻，加入蟹肉、銀芽及魚翅混合。
3. 燒熱油，傾入上述材料，灒紹酒，拌炒蛋液至散碎及將乾透，澆入凍開水，炒至蛋液乾身，上碟。

1. Add oil into a hot wok. Stir-fry mung bean sprouts thoroughly. Add seasoning (1) and stir-fry well. Drain.
2. Whisk eggs and seasoning (2). Mix in crabmeat, mung bean sprouts and shark's fin.
3. Heat oil in wok. Pour in the ingredients from step (2). Sizzle in Shaoxing wine. Stir-fry the egg mixture until breaks into bits and almost dry in texture. Add cold drinking water and stir-fry until dry. Serve.

蟹 粉 獅 子 頭

Crab Roe and Pork Balls with White Cabbage

材料 Ingredients

鮮蟹肉 2 兩
蟹膏適量
半肥瘦豬肉 4 兩
去皮馬蹄 2 個
小棠菜 4 兩
薑 2 片

75 g fresh crabmeat
crab roe
150 g half fat and half lean pork
2 peeled water chestnuts
150 g Shanghainese white cabbages
2 slices ginger

調味料 Seasoning >1

鹽及糖各 1/4 茶匙
生抽半湯匙
麻油及胡椒粉各少許
水 2 湯匙
生粉 1 湯匙

1/4 tsp salt
1/4 tsp sugar
1/2 tbsp light soy sauce
sesame oil
ground white pepper
2 tbsps water
1 tbsp caltrop starch

調味料 Seasoning >2

清雞湯 125 毫升
清水 25 毫升
糖 1/4 茶匙
老抽 1 茶匙

125 ml chicken broth
25 ml water
1/4 tsp sugar
1 tsp dark soy sauce

生粉獻（拌勻）
Caltrop starch solution (mixed well)

水 1 湯匙
生粉 1 茶匙

1 tbsp water
1 tsp caltrop starch

準備工夫 Preparation

- 將肉蟹 1 隻（約 14 兩）洗淨，取出蟹膏；蟹身隔水蒸約 13 分鐘，待凍，拆蟹肉約 2 至 3 兩。
- 馬蹄用刀面拍碎，剁成幼粒。
- 半肥瘦豬肉剁碎，與蟹肉、蟹膏、馬蹄及調味料（1）拌勻，搓成 4 個獅子頭肉丸。
- 小棠菜開邊，洗淨備用。
- Rinse 1 mud crab (about 525 g) and take the crab roe. Steam the crab for about 13 minutes and set aside to let cool. Shell and bone to take about 75 g to 113 g of crabmeat.
- Pat water chestnuts with a knife and chop into fine dices.
- Chop pork and mix with crabmeat, crab roe, water chestnuts and seasoning (1). Knead the mixture into 4 round balls.
- Cut white cabbages into two halves along the length. Rinse and set aside.

做法 Method

1. 獅子頭肉丸用油半煎炸至表面硬身，盛起。
2. 燒熱砂鍋下油，爆香薑片，放入小棠菜，注入調味料（2）拌勻，排上獅子頭肉丸煮約 8 分鐘，埋獻，上碟品嘗。

1. Shallow-fry the pork balls with oil until the surfaces are hard in texture. Drain.
2. Heat oil in a clay pot. Stir-fry ginger slices until fragrant. Add white cabbages. Mix in seasoning (2). Arrange the pork balls into the pot and cook for about 8 minutes. Thicken with the caltrop starch solution. Serve.

醉 花 蟹
Drunken Coral Crab with Shaoxing Wine

材料 Ingredients

花蟹 1 隻（約 12 兩）
薑 3 片
葱 4 條
紹酒 250 毫升

1 coral crab (about 450 g)
3 slices ginger
4 sprigs spring onion
250 ml Shaoxing wine

調味料 Seasoning

泰國魚露 250 毫升
清水 400 毫升
糖 6 湯匙

250 ml Thai fish gravy
400 ml water
6 tbsps sugar

汁料內為何加入魚露？

Why add fish gravy into the sauce for soaking crab?

更能提升蟹肉之鮮味，成為薰香醉人之冷盤，令人百吃不厭！

Fish gravy can further enhance the taste of crabmeat, it makes this cold dish always tastes good!

除花蟹外，還可選用哪類蟹？

What kind of crab can be used except coral crab?

肉蟹也適合製成醉蟹，蟹肉滲滿酒香味！

Mud crab can also be used.

花蟹買回來不立即炮製，如何養活？

How to raise coral crab if not cooked immediately after bought?

將花蟹（連繩）放於碟上，用濕布蓋着，可養活大半天。

Put the crab (with strings) on a plate and cover with a damp cloth. It can live for more than half day.

準備工夫 Preparation

- 煮滾調味料，待涼，加入紹酒拌成汁料。
- 花蟹去除內臟，刷洗乾淨，瀝乾水分。
- Bring seasoning to the boil and set aside to let cool. Mix with Shaoxing wine to become the sauce.
- Remove entrails from coral crab. Rub and wash thoroughly. Rinse and drain.

做法 Method

1. 花蟹、薑及葱同放碟內，隔水蒸約 14 分鐘至蟹全熟，待涼。
2. 蟹斬件，略拍蟹鉗，放入紹酒汁料內浸泡，冷藏 2 小時即可享用。

1. Put coral crab, ginger and spring onion on a plate. Steam for about 14 minutes until done. Set aside to let cool.
2. Chop the crab into pieces. Pat the pincers briefly. Soak them into the wine sauce. Refrigerate for 2 hours and serve.

馬 介 休 蟹 肉 薯 球
Deep-fried Potato Balls with Bacalhau and Crabmeat

材料　Ingredients

鮮蟹肉 2 兩

馬介休 1 兩

馬鈴薯 10 兩

洋葱 1 兩

75 g fresh crabmeat

38 g Bacalhau (salted codfish)

375 g potatoes

38 g onion

調味料　Seasoning

鹽 1/4 茶匙

生抽 2 茶匙

胡椒粉少許

生粉 3 湯匙

1/4 tsp salt

2 tsps light soy sauce

ground white pepper

3 tbsps caltrop starch

甚麼是馬介休？哪裏有售？
What is Bacalhau? Where to buy it?

馬介休是葡萄牙之醃製食材，是鱈魚用鹽醃製而成，於澳門的乾貨店有售。
Bacalhau (in Portuguese) is a kind of pickled food from Portuguese. It is salted codfish and can be bought from grocery stores selling Macau products.

為何用薯絲炮製？
Why potato shreds are used?

咬入口，絲絲馬鈴薯質感，口感非常豐富！
They enhance the texture of the dish.

馬介休之鹹味會掩蓋蟹肉之鮮味嗎？
Would the salty taste of Bacalhau cover the fresh taste of crabmeat?

絕對不會，馬介休的鹹味較淡，1 兩的份量不會掩蓋蟹肉之鮮味。
No. Bacalhau has a light salty taste only and 38 g of it would not cover the fresh taste of crabmeat.

準備工夫 Preparation

- 馬介休抹淨，去骨、去皮，切幼粒。
- 馬鈴薯去皮，磨成幼絲。
- 洋葱切碎。
- Wipe Bacalhau. Bone and skin. Dice finely.
- Peel potatoes and grate into fine shreds.
- Chop onion.

做法 Method

1. 馬介休、薯絲、蟹肉、洋葱及調味料拌勻，搓成薯球（約 12 個）。
2. 燒熱油，下薯球炸至熟透及金黃香脆，上碟品嘗。

1. Mix Bacalhau, potato shreds, crabmeat, onion and seasoning. Knead into about 12 potato balls.
2. Heat oil in wok. Deep-fry the potato balls until done, golden brown and crispy. Serve hot.

川 醬 辣 蟹 銀 絲 煲
Sichuan Spicy Crab and Vermicelli in Clay Pot

如何烹調得更健康？
How to cook this dish in a healthy way?

蟹件用半煎炸之方式代替泡油，既可節省食油，又令身體更健康。

Shallow-fry the crab instead of blanching it in oil not only saves oil but also healthier for the body.

這道菜帶四川風味嗎？
Is this dish in Sichuan style?

豆瓣醬配搭辣椒乾炒蟹，香辣味濃，具四川辣菜之特色。

Stir-frying crab with spicy soybean sauce and dried chili gives rich hot taste. It is also the characteristic of Sichuan spicy dishes.

材料 Ingredients
肉蟹 1 隻（約 1 斤）
乾粉絲 1 1/4 兩（50 克）
豆瓣醬 1 湯匙
辣椒乾 1 隻
薑 2 片
蒜茸 1 湯匙
葱 1 條
生粉適量

1 mud crab (about 600 g)
50 g dried vermicelli
1 tbsp spicy soybean sauce
1 dried chili
2 slices ginger
1 tbsp minced garlic
1 sprig spring onion
caltrop starch

調味料 Seasoning
上湯 1 1/3 杯
鹽 1/3 茶匙

1 1/3 cups broth
1/3 tsp salt

做法　Method

1. 蟹件灑上生粉，用適量油半煎炸至蟹件轉成紅色，盛起。

2. 燒熱瓦鍋，下油爆香豆瓣醬、辣椒乾、薑片及蒜茸，加入蟹件，注入調味料煮滾 6 分鐘，加入粉絲多煮 2 分鐘，下葱段再煮片刻，原鍋上桌品嘗。

1. Sprinkle caltrop starch over the crab. Shallow-fry in oil until turns red colour and drain.

2. Heat clay pot and add oil. Stir-fry spicy soybean sauce, dried chili, ginger slices and minced garlic quickly until fragrant. Add the crab and pour in seasoning. Cook for 6 minutes. Put in the vermicelli and cook for 2 minutes more. Add sectioned spring onion and cook for a while. Serve.

Cookery Lesson 3   >4 人份量

椰 皇 蟹 肉 钵 仔 蛋
Steamed Eggs and Coconut Juice with Crabmeat

材料 Ingredients

鮮蟹肉 2 兩
椰皇 1 個
雞蛋 4 個
芫茜適量

75 g fresh crabmeat
1 king coconut
4 eggs
coriander

調味料 Seasoning

鹽半茶匙

1/2 tsp salt

用具 Tool

瓦缽 1 個（18 厘米）

1 clay saucer bowl (18 cm)

用瓦缽蒸蛋有何技巧？
What's the technique of steaming eggs in saucer bowl?

由於瓦缽傳熱速度較慢，因此蒸首 4 分鐘時，建議使用中大火。
Since clay saucer bowl is slow in heat transmission, it is suggested to use medium-high heat at the first 4 minutes of steaming.

蒸蛋與椰皇水混和，食味如何？
What's the taste of steaming eggs together with coconut juice?

蛋內散發陣陣清新的椰皇香氣，配上鮮甜的蟹肉，確是另一番味覺享受！
The coconut aroma gets into the eggs thus it is a great experience to serve it with fresh and sweet crabmeat.

甚麼是此餸成功之要訣？
What's the hint to make this dish successfully?

必須將椰水及雞蛋完全拌勻，否則難以蒸熟。
The coconut juice and eggs must be mixed well completely, or it is hard to be steamed until done.

- 刺穿椰皇頂部之洞,傾出 250 毫升椰水,備用。
- Pinch through the hole at the top part of king coconut. Pour out 250 ml of coconut juice and set aside.

做法 Method

1. 雞蛋及調味料拂勻,與椰皇水拌勻,傾入瓦缽內,用中大火隔水蒸 4 分鐘。
2. 蛋面鋪上鮮蟹肉,再蒸 3 分鐘,加入芫茜,加蓋稍焗即可。

1. Whisk eggs with seasoning. Mix eggs with coconut juice and pour into a saucer bowl. Steam over medium-high heat for 4 minutes.
2. Lay fresh crabmeat over the surface of eggs and steam for 3 minutes more. Put in coriander and cover the lid for a while. Serve.

鹽 香 豆 瓣 奄 仔 蟹
Stir-fried Small Green Crabs with Spicy Soybean Sauce

甚麼是奄仔蟹？
What are small green crabs?

⬇

是肉蟹及膏蟹之幼蟹，色澤較淺，奄仔小，故稱為「奄仔蟹」，無論蟹肉及蟹膏，同樣鮮甜嫩滑！

Small green crabs are young mud crabs and young coral crabs. Though light in color and small in size, their crabmeat and crab roe are also sweet and smooth.

可用哪款醬料代替豆瓣醬？
Which kind of sauce can be used to replace spicy soybean sauce?

⬇

柱候醬也是另一款不錯的選擇，適合不嗜辣者。

Chu Hou sauce is a good choice for those who do not prefer spicy taste.

準備工夫 Preparation
- 奄仔蟹洗淨，去內臟，斬件。
- 乾葱切片。
- Rinse small green crabs. Remove the entrails and chop into pieces.
- Slice shallots.

材料 Ingredients
奄仔蟹 2 隻（約 12 兩）
乾葱 2 粒
蒜茸 1 湯匙
豆瓣醬 4 茶匙
生粉適量
紹酒 1 湯匙

2 small green crabs (about 450 g)
2 shallots
1 tbsp minced garlic
4 tsps spicy soybean sauce
caltrop starch
1 tbsp Shaoxing wine

調味料 Seasoning
鹽 1 茶匙
五香粉 1/3 茶匙
水 8 湯匙

1 tsp salt
1/3 tsp five-spice powder
8 tbsps water

做法 Method
1. 蟹件灑上生粉，放入熱油內泡油，盛起。
2. 熱鑊下油，加入乾葱片、蒜茸及豆瓣醬爆香，下蟹件，灒紹酒及調味料，加蓋煮 6 分鐘即成。

1. Sprinkle caltrop starch over the crabs. Blanch in hot oil and drain.
2. Add oil into a hot wok. Stir-fry shallot slices, minced garlic and spicy soybean sauce quickly until fragrant. Add the crabs. Pour in Shaoxing wine and seasoning. Cover the lid and cook for 6 minutes. Serve.

香茅辣椒炒東風螺
Stir-fried Spiral Babylon with Lemongrass and Chilies

材料　Ingredients

東風螺 1 斤
香茅 2 枝
指天椒 3 至 4 隻
蒜頭 1 粒

600 g spiral babylon
2 stalks lemongrass
3 to 4 bird's eye chilies
1 clove garlic

調味料　Seasoning

清水 2/3 杯
鹽 2/3 茶匙
糖半茶匙
老抽半湯匙
魚露 3/4 湯匙
生粉 1 茶匙

2/3 cup water
2/3 tsps salt
1/2 tsp sugar
1/2 tbsp dark soy sauce
3/4 tbsp fish gravy
1 tsp caltrop starch

COOKERY FORUM

此菜可以作為頭盤冷吃嗎？

Can this dish become a cold appetiter?

⬇

絕對可以，建議可預早一天烹調，適當冷藏，食味更佳。

Absolutely. It is suggested to cook a day in advance and store in the refrigerator.

為甚麼東風螺先飛水才炒煮？

Why scald the spiral babylon before stir-frying?

⬇

令附在螺身的雜質掉落水中，去掉雜質，食用時更健康。

This method can remove any impurities in the spiral babylon.

若不吃辣，可減掉指天椒嗎？味道有影響嗎？

Can the bird's eye chilies be removed if I do not prefer spicy taste? Would the taste of the dish be affected?

⬇

當然可以，不過味道略遜。

Of course, but the flavor reduces a bit.

準備工夫 Preparation

- 東風螺洗淨，用淡鹽水浸 1 小時或以上（有助吐沙），烹調時再清洗一次。
- 香茅斜切成段；指天椒切小片；蒜頭切片。
- Rinse spiral babylon. Soak in diluted salted water for 1 hour or above to let them spit out sand. Rinse once again before cooking.
- Section lemongrass at an angle. Cut bird's eye chilies into small slices. Slice garlic.

做法 Method

1. 煮滾一鍋水，放入東風螺飛水 2 分鐘，盛起。
2. 燒熱適量油，下蒜片、香茅及辣椒炒香，注入調味料煮滾片刻，加入東風螺拌炒至汁液濃稠，上碟享用。

1. Bring a pot of water to the boil. Scald spiral babylon for 2 minutes and drain.
2. Heat oil in a wok. Stir-fry garlic slices, lemongrass and chilies until fragrant. Pour in the seasoning and boil for a while. Add spiral babylon and stir-fry until the sauce thickens. Serve.

XO 醬 煎 金 蠔
Fried Golden Dried Oysters with XO Sauce

甚麼是薑汁酒？可用紹酒代替嗎？
What is ginger wine? Can it be replaced with Shaoxing wine?

薑汁酒是薑汁與紹酒混和，比例為 1 比 1。潷入薑汁酒，可辟除金蠔的腥味。

Ginger wine is made by mixing ginger juice and Shaoxing wine in a 1:1 ratio. It can remove the fishy smell of golden dried oyster.

甚麼是金蠔？
What is golden dried oyster?

金蠔是指曬至半乾濕之大蠔豉，海味店有售。

Golden dried oyster is big oyster dried under the sun until medium dried. It can be bought from shops selling Chinese dried seafood stuff.

金蠔需要特別處理方法嗎？
Do golden dried oysters require special handling?

不同店舖售賣的金蠔，軟硬程度有別，處理方法也不同：肉質較硬的金蠔，宜先蒸後才烹調；較軟身的金蠔，洗淨後即可煎熟食用。

Golden dried oysters sold at different shops have different levels of hardness and thus require different handling ways. Harder golden dried oysters should be steamed before cooking; those soft in texture can be fried until done after rinsed.

材料 Ingredients

金蠔 8 隻，XO 醬 1 湯匙，薑汁酒 1 湯匙
8 golden dried oysters, 1 tbsp XO sauce, 1 tbsp ginger wine

調味料 Seasoning

清水 4 湯匙，生抽半茶匙，蜜糖 1 茶匙
4 tbsps water, 1/2 tsp light soy sauce, 1 tsp honey

準備工夫 Preparation

- 金蠔洗淨，吸乾水分。
- Rinse golden dried oysters and wipe dry.

做法 Method

1. 熱鑊下油，放入金蠔煎至兩面金黃色，盛起。
2. 燒熱油，下 XO 醬炒香，加入金蠔，潷薑汁酒，注入調味料用小火煮至汁液濃稠，上碟享用。

1. Add oil into a hot wok. Fry golden dried oysters until both sides are golden and set aside.
2. Heat oil in wok. Stir-fry XO sauce until fragrant. Add the golden dried oysters and pour in ginger wine at the side lightly. Put in the seasoning and cook over low heat until the sauce thickens. Serve.

十 穀 米 釀 鮮 魷 筒
Baked Stuffed Squid with Ten-grain Rice

COOKERY FORUM

為何十穀米加鹽煮熟？
Why cooking ten-grain rice with salt?

令十穀米帶淡淡味道，不致寡淡無味。
This makes the ten-grain rice has a light flavor.

釀鮮魷筒有何秘訣？
What's the tip of stuffing fillings into fresh squid?

將十穀米釀入鮮魷筒時，米飯不可鬆散，否則切件時，飯粒容易散開。
The ten-grain rice to be stuffed into fresh squid cannot be scattered or loosed, or the rice scatters when the squid is cut into pieces.

材料　Ingredients

鮮魷 1 隻（12 兩，約 25 厘米長）
十穀米 3 兩
蒜茸 1 茶匙
清水 225 毫升

1 fresh squid
(450 g and about 25 cm long)
113 g ten-grain rice
1 tsp minced garlic
225 ml water

醃汁　Marinade

鰻魚汁 2 湯匙
黑胡椒碎 1 茶匙
蒜茸半湯匙
麻油少許

2 tbsps eel sauce
1 tsp chopped black pepper
1/2 tbsp minced garlic
sesame oil

調味料　Seasoning

鹽 1/3 茶匙

1/3 tsp salt

蘸汁　Dipping sauce

水 2 湯匙
生粉半茶匙
餘下的醃汁

2 tbsps water
1/2 tsp caltrop starch
remaining marinade sauce

準備工夫 Preparation

- 鮮魷撕去外衣，取出鮮魷鬚及軟骨，洗淨，抹乾魷魚筒內外，保持圓筒狀。
- 醃汁拌勻，均勻地塗抹在鮮魷兩面，醃 1 小時。
- 十穀米洗淨，用清水浸 2 小時，加入調味料拌勻煮熟，待涼。
- 預熱焗爐 200 ℃。
- Tease outer skin from fresh squid and remove tentacles and soft bones. Rinse and wipe dry its inside and outside. Keep its cylindrical shape.
- Mix the marinade and rub over the two sides of fresh squid evenly. Set aside for 1 hour.
- Rinse ten-grain rice and soak in water for 2 hours. Mix in seasoning and cook until done. Set aside to let cool.
- Preheat an oven to 200°C.

做法 Method

1. 十穀米飯釀入鮮魷筒內至 7 至 8 成滿，用牙籤封口。
2. 焗盆鋪上錫紙，放上鮮魷筒焗 8 分鐘，取出，塗上餘下之醃汁，再焗 8 分鐘，切件，上碟。
3. 下油爆香蒜茸，加入蘸汁材料煮滾，伴鮮魷筒享用。

1. Stuff ten-grain rice into fresh squid until medium-well full and fix the end with toothpick.
2. Lay aluminum foil over a baking tray. Put in the squid and bake for 8 minutes. Rub over the remaining marinade and bake for 8 minutes more. Cut into pieces and put on a plate.
3. Heat oil in a wok and stir-fry minced garlic until fragrant. Add the ingredients of the dipping sauce and bring to the boil. Serve with fresh squid at the side.

金 不 換 蒸 鮮 帶 子

Steamed Fresh Scallops with Basil Leaves

材料 Ingredients

鮮薄殼帶子 8 隻
金不換 1 棵
蒜茸 1 1/2 湯匙
乾葱茸 1 湯匙
紅辣椒絲 1 湯匙

8 fresh thin-shelled scallops
1 stalk basil leaves
1 1/2 tbsps minced garlic
1 tbsp minced shallot
1 tbsp red chili shreds

調味料 Seasoning

生抽 1 湯匙
老抽 1 湯匙
糖半湯匙
麻油 1 茶匙
水半湯匙

1 tbsp light soy sauce
1 tbsp dark soy sauce
1/2 tbsp sugar
1 tsp sesame oil
1/2 tbsp water

最後放入金不換葉，香氣足夠滲入帶子嗎？
Can the smell of basil leaves go into the scallops if putting in at the last?

金不換不宜久煮，故最後放入稍焗即散發芳香之味。
Basil leaves cannot be cooked for a long time. Thus putting in at the last step and cover the lid for a while, it can bring out their aroma already.

如何修剪帶子薄殼？
How to trim the thin shells of scallops?

沿帶子殼適度修剪，排碟及食用更方便。
Trim around the shells so that they are easier for arranging on the plate and more convenient for consumption.

哪裏購買金不換？
Where to buy basil leaves?

泰國雜貨店或部份菜檔均有出售。
They can be bought from Thai grocery stores and some vegetable stalls.

準備工夫 Preparation

- 金不換摘出葉片，洗淨備用。
- 用小刀打開帶子外殼，去腸及去內臟，修剪帶子薄殼，洗淨，瀝乾水分，排於碟上。
- Tear off leaves from basil. Rinse and set aside.
- Open the shells of scallops with a knife. Remove entrails. Trim their thin shells. Rinse and drain. Arrange scallops on a plate.

做法 Method

1. 熱鑊下油，爆香蒜茸、乾葱茸及紅椒絲，待涼，鋪在帶子上。
2. 隔水蒸約 3 至 4 分鐘，灑入金不換葉，稍焗片刻。
3. 分別煮滾少許生油及調味料，依次澆在帶子上，趁熱品嘗。

1. Add oil into a hot wok. Stir-fry minced garlic, minced shallot and shredded red chili until fragrant. Set aside to let cool and arrange onto the scallops.
2. Steam for about 3 to 4 minutes. Sprinkle over basil leaves and cover the lid for a while.
3. Bring a little oil and seasoning to the boil respectively. Pour them over the scallops in order. Serve hot.

海 膽 蒸 蛋 白
Steamed Sea Urchin with Egg White

哪裏購買海膽？
Where to buy sea urchin?

一般大型超級市場或日式壽司店均有出售，價錢相宜。

It can be bought from large supermarkets or Japanese sushi stores with reasonable price.

如何蒸得嫩滑的蛋白？
How to make smooth and soft steamed egg white?

火候勿太大，先用中火再調至慢火蒸熟；或蓋上耐熱保鮮紙，均可蒸成嫩滑的蛋白。

The heat must not be high. Steam over medium heat first then turn to low heat and cook until done. Or cover the container with heat-resistant cling wrap.

海膽買回來後，需要特別處理嗎？
Does the sea urchin require special handling after purchase?

毋須特別處理，緊記放於雪櫃冷藏，取海膽時務必謹慎，因海膽容易斷爛。

No, just remember to refrigerate it and take it carefully since it breaks easily.

材料 Ingredients
海膽 40 克
蛋白 4 個（200 毫升）
葱花適量

40 g sea urchin
4 egg whites (200 ml)
diced spring onion

調味料 Seasoning
鹽 1/3 茶匙
清雞湯 200 毫升

1/3 tsp salt
200 ml chicken broth

準備工夫 Preparation
- 取半份海膽壓成茸；其餘半份留用。
- Crush half portion of sea urchin and set aside the other half.

做法 Method
1. 海膽茸、蛋白及調味料拌勻，傾入深碟內。
2. 隔水用中火蒸 3 分鐘，轉小火再蒸約 4 分鐘，排入餘下之海膽，灑上葱花，續蒸片刻即成。

1. Whisk egg white with crushed sea urchin and seasoning. Mix well and pour into a deep plate.
2. Steam over medium heat for 3 minutes. Turn to low heat and steam for about 4 minutes. Arrange in the remaining sea urchin. Sprinkle in diced spring onion and steam for a while. Serve.

瑤 柱 汁 燴 鮮 鮑

Braised Abalones with Dried Scallops Extract

材料 Ingredients

大連鮮鮑魚 8 隻（約 14 兩），
乾瑤柱 1 兩，葱段 6 條，薑絲 1
湯匙，紹酒 1 湯匙
8 Dalian fresh abalones (about
525 g), 38 g dried scallops, 6
sectioned spring onion, 1 tbsp
shredded ginger, 1 tbsp Shaoxing
wine

調味料 Seasoning

瑤柱汁 5 湯匙，鹽 1/4 茶匙，糖
1/4 茶匙，生粉 3/4 茶匙
5 tbsps dried scallops extract,
1/4 tsp salt, 1/4 tsp sugar, 3/4 tsp
caltrop starch

COOKERY FORUM

大連鮮鮑魚價錢昂貴嗎？
Are Dalian fresh abalones expensive?

▼

大連鮮鮑魚屬中價海鮮，一斤售大約港幣 120 元至 130 元，每斤之數量視乎鮑魚大小而定。

They belongs to medium priced seafood with about HK$120 to $130 for one catty (600 g). The number of abalones for one catty depends on the size of abalones.

選用大顆瑤柱或小顆的，對食味有影響嗎？
What size of dried scallops should be used and would the taste of the dish be affected?

▼

只要是質素佳之瑤柱，瑤柱碎也絕無問題。

Use good-quality dried scallops and even fragments of dried scallops can do.

準備工夫 Preparation

- 乾瑤柱沖淨，用溫水 9 湯匙浸 2 小時，取出，與紹酒 1 湯匙拌勻，隔水蒸 45 分鐘，預留瑤柱汁 5 湯匙，瑤柱待涼，取部分瑤柱拆絲（約 2 湯匙）。
- 鮮鮑魚連殼刷洗乾淨，用廚房剪刀起出鮑魚肉，去內臟，洗淨，抹乾水分，排回殼內。
- 葱段切絲備用。
- Rinse dried scallops and soak in 9 tbsps of warm water for 2 hours. Drain and mix well with 1 tbsp of Shaoxing wine. Steam for 45 minutes. Reserve 5 tbsps of the dried scallops extract. Set the dried scallops aside to let cool. Tear some dried scallops into shreds (about 2 tbsps).
- Wash and brush fresh abalones with their shells. Take up the abalones with a pair of kitchen scissors. Remove entrails. Rinse and wipe dry. Put the abalones on the shells.
- Shred spring onion and set aside.

做法 Method

1. 鮑魚排於碟上，薑絲及葱絲放在鮑魚上，用大火蒸 6 分鐘，取出。
2. 煮滾少許油及調味料，拌勻，下瑤柱絲拌勻，澆在鮑魚上品嘗。

1. Put abalones on a plate. Put ginger shreds and spring onion shreds over the abalones. Steam over high heat for 6 minutes.
2. Bring a little oil and seasoning to the boil. Mix well and add dried scallops shreds. Pour over the abalones and serve.

金盞海鮮燴
Braised Seafood and Zucchini in Golden Cup

炸金盞容易處理嗎？

Is it easy to deep-fry golden cup?

雲吞皮輕輕地包在甘筍上，放入熱油內，雲吞皮迅速炸至香脆及脫開，處理簡易，緊記油溫不要過熱。

Wrap wanton wrapper around the carrot and deep-fry in hot oil. The wrapper becomes crispy and demould quickly. The steps are simple but remember that the oil cannot be too hot.

預備及烹調時間需時多久？

What are the preparation and cooking time?

預備時間約 20 分鐘；烹調時間約 10 分鐘，耗時不多。

The preparation time is about 20 minutes while the cooking time is about 10 minutes.

材料 Ingredients

中蝦 8 隻
急凍帶子 4 隻
鮮蟹肉 3 兩
魚柳 3 兩
翠玉瓜 4 兩
方型大雲吞皮 8 張
蒜茸半湯匙
甘筍 1 條（直徑不超過 5 厘米）

8 medium-sized prawns
4 frozen scallops
113 g fresh crabmeat
113 g fish fillet
150 g zucchini
8 square large wanton wrappers
1/2 tbsp minced garlic
1 carrot (diameter not exceeds 5 cm)

醃料 Marinade>1

鹽 1/4 茶匙
胡椒粉少許

1/4 tsp salt
ground white pepper

醃料 Marinade >2

鹽 1/3 茶匙
胡椒粉及麻油各少許
蛋白 1 茶匙
生粉半湯匙

1/3 tsp salt
ground white pepper
sesame oil
1 tsp egg white
1/2 tbsp caltrop starch

調味料 Seasoning

鹽半茶匙
水適量

1/2 tsp salt
water

獻汁（拌勻）
Thickening sauce(mixed well)

水 1/4 杯
鹽及糖各 1/4 茶匙
生抽半茶匙
麻油少許
生粉半茶匙

1/4 cup water
1/4 tsp salt
1/4 tsp sugar
1/2 tsp light soy sauce
sesame oil
1/2 tsp caltrop starch

準備工夫 Preparation

- 甘筍洗淨及抹乾水分。
- 燒熱油 1 杯（見出現小泡沫即可），在甘筍較粗一端包上雲吞皮，放入油內炸至金黃色及香脆的金盞，脫開甘筍，放於碟上。
- 中蝦去殼、去腸，洗淨，抹乾後與醃料（1）拌勻。
- 帶子解凍，每隻切為兩份；魚柳切粗粒；帶子、魚柳及醃料（2）拌勻醃 10 分鐘。
- 煮滾適量清水，下帶子浸 1 分鐘，盛起。
- Rinse and wipe dry carrot.
- Heat a cup of oil in wok (until little bubbles appear). Wrap wanton wrapper at the thicker side of carrot. Deep-fry in oil until golden brown. This becomes crispy golden cup. Remove the carrot and put the cup on a plate.
- Shell and devein prawns. Rinse and wipe dry. Mix well with marinade (1).
- Defrost scallops and each cut into 2 pieces. Cut fish fillet into thick dices. Mix scallops and fish fillet with marinade (2) and set aside for 10 minutes.
- Bring water to the boil. Add scallops and soak for 1 minute. Drain.

做法 Method

1. 翠玉瓜洗淨，切粗粒，與調味料炒熟，盛起。
2. 熱鑊下油，加入中蝦、魚柳及帶子，下蒜茸拌炒至香氣四溢，最後加入蟹肉、獻汁及翠玉瓜炒勻，分放入金盞內享用。

1. Rinse zucchini and cut into thick dices. Stir-fry with seasoning until done and set aside.
2. Add oil into a hot wok. Put in prawns, fish fillet and scallops. Add minced garlic and stir-fry until fragrant. Pour in crabmeat, thickening sauce and zucchini. Stir-fry well and put into the golden cups. Serve.

椰 皇 海 鮮 焗 飯
Baked Seafood Rice in King Coconut

材料　Ingredients

椰皇 4 個
白飯 8 兩
蝦仁 3 兩
魚柳 3 兩
急凍帶子（厚身）3 隻
菜莖 3 兩
甘筍 1 兩
椰皇肉適量
乾葱片 1 湯匙
紗紙 1 張

4 king coconuts
300 g cooked rice
113 g shelled prawns
113 g fish fillet
3 frozen scallops (thick flesh)
113 g vegetable stalks
38 g carrot
flesh from king coconuts
1 tbsp sliced shallot
1 sheet unbleached mulberry paper

醃料　Marinade

鹽 2/3 茶匙
胡椒粉少許

2/3 tsp salt
ground white pepper

調味料　Seasoning

椰水 3 湯匙
鹽 3/4 茶匙
蠔油半湯匙

3 tbsps coconut juice
3/4 tsp salt
1/2 tbsp oyster sauce

可選用哪類魚及蔬菜，作為魚柳及菜莖材料？
Which kind of fish and what kind of vegetable stalks should be used?

魚柳可選用斑肉、青衣或龍脷柳；菜莖可用西蘭花莖、菜心莖、芥蘭莖或西芹。
For the fish, grouper, green wrasse or sole fillet can be chosen. For the vegetable, stalks of broccoli, choy sum, kale or celery can be used.

炒海鮮飯有何竅門？
What's the tip of stir-frying seafood rice?

必須使用適中的火力炒飯，勿將飯粒炒燶，影響賣相。
Stir-fry rice over medium heat so that the rice does not become charred.

海鮮焗飯的味道如何？
What's the taste of baked seafood rice?

海鮮飯滲有陣陣椰皇淡香，伴海鮮同吃，味道絕對吸引！
The seafood rice comes with light coconut smell and it tastes good with the seafood.

準備工夫 Preparation

- 將椰皇頂部約 4 厘米橫剁成椰蓋（售者可代勞），傾出椰水留用；刮出少許椰肉，切碎備用。
- 蝦仁去腸，洗淨;魚柳切粒;帶子解凍，沖淨。
- 甘筍及菜莖切粒，放入滾水內灼熟。
- 蝦仁、魚柳及帶子抹乾水分，加入醃料醃 10 分鐘，飛水，取出，帶子切粒。
- 預熱焗爐 180℃；紗紙剪成 4 張。
- Cut off top part of king coconuts at about 4 cm position to become the cover (or ask the monger for help). Set aside the coconut juice. Scrape out a little coconut flesh and finely chop.
- Devein shelled prawns and rinse. Dice fish fillet. Defrost scallops and rinse.
- Dice carrot and vegetable stalks. Blanch in boiling water until done.
- Wipe dry shelled prawns, fish fillet and scallops. Marinate for 10 minutes. Scald and drain. Dice the scallops.
- Preheat an oven to 180°C. Cut unbleached mulberry paper into 4 pieces.

做法 Method

1. 燒熱油，下乾葱片炒香，加入白飯、海鮮粒、菜莖、甘筍、椰皇肉及調味料徹底拌炒。
2. 將椰皇海鮮飯分成 4 份，放入椰皇內，加上椰皇蓋，包上紗紙，放入焗爐焗 20 分鐘，取出品嘗。

1. Heat oil in wok. Stir-fry sliced shallot until fragrant. Add cooked rice, diced seafood, vegetable stalks, carrot, coconut flesh and seasoning. Stir-fry thoroughly.
2. Divide the stir-fried seafood rice into 4 portions and put into the king coconuts. Put on the covers and wrap with unbleached mulberry paper. Bake in the oven for 20 minutes and serve.

鮑汁金銀帶子

Fried Scallops with Abalone Sauce and Dried Scallop Shreds

材料 Ingredients

急凍大帶子 8 隻
乾瑤柱 2 粒
鮑魚汁 1 湯匙
紹酒 1 茶匙

8 frozen large scallops
2 dried scallops
1 tbsp abalone sauce
1 tsp Shaoxing wine

醃料 Marinade

鹽 1/4 茶匙
胡椒粉少許
生粉半茶匙
清雞湯適量

1/4 tsp salt
ground white pepper
1/2 tsp caltrop starch
chicken broth

選用哪款帶子較合適？

Which kind of scallop should be used?

▼

建議選買日本北海道帶子，烹調後不會收縮。

It is suggested to buy Japanese Hokkaido scallops that would not shrink after cooked.

帶子醃製後，為何放入清雞湯內略浸？

Why soak scallops in chicken broth after marinated?

▼

帶子略浸清雞湯，能保持其形狀，而且減省煎帶子的時間，以免影響肉質變韌。

Soaking scallops in chicken broth briefly can keep their shapes and also reduce their cooking time. Their texture are not affected.

調味料 Seasoning

瑤柱汁 3 湯匙（若份量不足，可加水）
糖半茶匙
老抽 1 茶匙
麻油少許
生粉半茶匙

3 tbsps dried scallops extract
(add water if the amount obtained
is not enough)
1/2 tsp sugar
1 tsp dark soy sauce
sesame oil
1/2 tsp caltrop starch

準備工夫 Preparation

- 乾瑤柱沖淨，用暖水預浸 2 小時，取出，與紹酒拌勻隔水蒸 45 分鐘（瑤柱汁留用），待涼後拆絲，用油炸脆。

- 帶子解凍，沖淨抹乾，加入醃料（清雞湯除外）拌勻醃 15 分鐘，放入燒熱的清雞湯內略浸（以浸過帶子面為宜），盛起，吸乾水分。

- Rinse dried scallops and soak in warm water for 2 hours. Drain and mix with Shaoxing wine. Steam for 45 minutes and reserve the extract. Set steamed dried scallops aside to let cool. Tear into shreds. Deep-fry the shreds in oil until crispy.

- Defrost scallops. Rinse and wipe dry. Mix with the marinade (except chicken broth) and set aside for 15 minutes. Soak in hot chicken broth briefly (covers the surface of the scallops). Drain and wipe dry.

做法 Method

1. 燒熱油，下帶子用慢火煎香兩面，上碟。

2. 煮滾鮑魚汁及調味料，澆在帶子上，灑入已炸脆之瑤柱絲即成。

1. Heat oil in wok. Fry scallops over low heat until both sides are fragrant. Put on a plate.

2. Bring abalone sauce and seasoning to the boil. Pour over the scallops. Sprinkle over deep-fried dried scallop shreds and serve.

黑 椒 醬 爆 蟶 子 皇
Stir-fried King Razor Clams with Black Pepper Sauce

材料 Ingredients

蟶子皇 8 隻（約 1 1/2 斤）	8 king razor clams (about 900 g)
指天椒 2 隻	2 bird's eye chilies
蒜茸 1 湯匙	1 tbsp minced garlic
薑米 2 茶匙	2 tsps chopped ginger
黑胡椒碎 4 茶匙	4 tsps chopped black pepper
葱絲 1 湯匙	1 tbsp shredded spring onion

COOKERY FORUM

如何挑選蟶子皇？

How to choose king razor clams?

選鮮活及體型大的蟶子為佳，肉多汁豐。

Choose fresh and large king razor clams that are fleshy and juicy.

蟶子肉容易炒至過韌嗎？

Would razor clams stir-fried to tough texture easily?

蟶子肉容易炒至韌，建議快手拌炒上碟。

Yes. You are suggested to stir-fry them quickly and serve.

調味料 Seasoning

水 4 湯匙
老抽 4 茶匙
鹽 1 茶匙
糖 半茶匙
胡椒粉少許
生粉 2 1/2 茶匙

4 tbsps water
4 tsps dark soy sauce
1 tsp salt
1/2 tsp sugar
ground white pepper
2 1/2 tsps caltrop starch

準備工夫 Preparation

- 剝開蟶子皇的薄膜，去腸臟（售者可代勞），洗淨。
- 指天椒切圈。
- Cut open thin membrane of king razor clams and remove the entrails (or ask the monger for help). Rinse.
- Cut bird's eye chilies into rings.

做法 Method

1. 煮滾適量清水（以浸過蟶子為宜），下蟶子略灼半分鐘，盛起，瀝乾水分。

2. 燒熱油爆香黑胡椒碎、紅椒圈、蒜茸及薑米，注入調味料煮滾，蟶子回鑊快速地炒勻，上碟，灑上葱絲裝飾即成。

1. Bring water to the boil (to cover all razor clams). Blanch razor clams briefly for about 30 seconds. Drain.

2. Heat oil in wok. Fry chopped black pepper, chili rings, minced garlic and chopped ginger until fragrant. Pour in seasoning and bring to the boil. Add the razor clams and stir-fry quickly. Put on a plate. Sprinkle over shredded spring onion for garnishing. Serve.

金 銀 蒜 蒸 象 拔 蚌 仔
Steamed Geoduck Clams with Garlic Duo

COOKERY FORUM

家裏沒有頭抽，怎辦？
What can I do if I do not have premium soy sauce?

可用生抽 1 湯匙及糖半茶匙煮溶代替。
You can cook 1 tbsp of light soy sauce and 1/2 tsp of sugar until dissolves to replace it.

象拔蚌仔蒸 4 分鐘熟透嗎？
Can geoduck clams be done by steaming 4 minutes only?

絕對熟透，增加烹調時間令肉質變韌，欠爽口的質感。
Absolutely. Increase the cooking time only makes them harder in texture and not crunchy.

象拔蚌於哪個季節有售？
Which season has large supply of geoduck clams?

街市海鮮檔通常於每年年尾至翌年初有售。
They are in large supply from the end of the year to the start of the next Chinese lunar year.

最後必須澆上熟油嗎？
Is it a must to pour over cooked oil at the last?

澆上熟油，令頭抽不直接滲入象拔蚌肉，以免鹹味太重。
Before you add premium soy sauce, pour over cooking oil first in order to avoid too heavy salty taste.

材料 Ingredients

象拔蚌仔 8 隻
蒜茸 3 湯匙
乾粉絲 1 兩
指天椒 3 隻
葱粒 1 湯匙

8 small geoduck clams
3 tbsps minced garlic
38 g dried vermicelli
3 bird's eye chilies
1 tbsp diced spring onion

調味料 Seasoning >1

清雞湯 125 毫升
125 ml chicken broth

調味料 Seasoning >2

鹽半茶匙
1/2 tsp salt

調味料 Seasoning >3

頭抽 1 湯匙
1 tbsp premium soy sauce

- 象拔蚌仔去掉腸臟（魚販可代勞），洗淨，瀝乾水分。
- 取 1/3 份量蒜茸炸香，備用。
- 燒熱清雞湯，下粉絲浸軟，剪成段。
- 指天椒切圈，用油及餘下之蒜茸炒香，下調味料（2）拌勻，待涼。
- Remove entrails from small geoduck clams (or ask the fishmonger for help). Rinse and drain.
- Deep-fry 1/3 portion of minced garlic until fragrant and set aside.
- Heat chicken broth and add vermicelli to soak until soft. Cut into sections.
- Cut bird's eye chilies into rings. Stir-fry with the remaining minced garlic and oil until fragrant. Put in seasoning (2) and mix well. Set aside to let cool.

做法 Method

1. 象拔蚌仔排於碟上，放上適量粉絲、香蒜及辣椒粒，隔水用中慢火蒸 4 分鐘，灑入葱粒，再蒸一會，取出。
2. 煮滾油 1 湯匙，澆在象拔蚌上，下調味料（3），灑入金蒜，趁熱享用。

1. Arrange small geoduck clams on a plate. Put in vermicelli, stir-fried minced garlic and diced chilies. Steam over medium-low heat for 4 minutes. Sprinkle over diced spring onion and steam for a while. Remove.
2. Bring 1 tbsp of oil to the boil. Pour over the small geoduck clams and add seasoning (3). Sprinkle over deep-fried minced garlic and serve hot.

沙 爹 雜 錦 海 鮮 串 燒

Baked Seafood Skewers with Satay Sauce

材料 Ingredients

中蝦 6 隻
急凍帶子 6 粒
鮮魷鬚 6 件
甜黃椒、甜青椒、甜紅椒各 6 片
竹籤 6 枝

6 medium-sized prawns
6 frozen scallops
6 fresh squid tentacles
6 slices yellow bell pepper
6 slices green bell pepper
6 slices red bell pepper
6 bamboo sticks

醃料 Marinade

沙爹醬半湯匙
黃薑粉 3/4 茶匙
鹽 1/3 茶匙
糖 1/3 茶匙
清水 2 1/2 湯匙
生粉 1 茶匙
油 1 湯匙

1/2 tbsp satay sauce
3/4 tsp turmeric powder
1/3 tsp salt
1/3 tsp sugar
2 1/2 tbsps water
1 tsp caltrop starch
1 tbsp oil

COOKERY FORUM

為何竹籤先浸水？
Why soak bamboo sticks in water first?

以免竹籤在焗爐內烤焗時燒焦。
This can avoid bamboo sticks get charred when baked in the oven.

哪裏購買黃薑粉？
Where to buy turmeric powder?

雜貨店或香料舖均有出售。
It can be bought from grocery stores or shops selling herbs.

有何烹調海鮮的小貼士？
What's the tip of cooking seafood?

所有海鮮醃製前，必須抹乾水分，以免影響醃味。
Wipe dry all seafood before marinating gives better taste.

蘸汁 Dipping sauce

沙爹醬 3 湯匙
糖半湯匙
魚露 1 湯匙
水 1 湯匙
炒香花生碎適量（後下）

3 tbsps satay sauce
1/2 tbsp sugar
1 tbsp fish gravy
1 tbsp water
stir-fried chopped peanut
(added at last)

- 竹籤浸水，備用。
- 中蝦去殼、去腸，洗淨，吸乾水分。
- 帶子解凍，去掉帶子枕，洗淨，抹乾水分。
- 鮮魷鬚洗淨，吸乾水分。
- 醃料拌勻，拌入三款海鮮料醃 20 分鐘。
- 預熱焗爐 200 ℃。
- Soak bamboo sticks in water and set aside.
- Shell and devein medium-sized prawns. Rinse and wipe dry.
- Defrost scallops and remove a white lump on the rim. Rinse and wipe dry.
- Rinse and wipe dry fresh squid tentacles.
- Mix well the marinade. Mix in three kinds of seafood and marinate for 20 minutes.
- Preheat an oven to 200°C.

做法 Method

1. 海鮮料及三色甜椒用竹籤相間地串起，放入焗爐烤焗約 10 分鐘。
2. 煮滾蘸汁，盛起，灑上花生碎，蘸海鮮串享用。

1. Skewer the seafood and bell peppers in sequence with bamboo sticks. Bake in the oven for about 10 minutes.
2. Bring the dipping sauce to the boil and sprinkle over chopped peanut. Serve with seafood skewers at the side.

銀絲香芹花蛤鍋

Clams with Vermicelli and Chinese Celery in Clay Pot

已用鹽水預浸花蛤，但花蛤仍藏沙粒，怎辦？
What can be done if clams still have sand after soaked in salted water?

用鹽水預浸花蛤及洗淨後，應乾淨無沙粒。若情況無改善，建議選擇到其他海鮮零售商購買。
Clams should be clean without sand after soaked in salted water and rinsed. If the situation cannot be improved, I suggest to buy clams at other seafood stalls.

花蛤可浸養至翌日才煮嗎？
Can clams be soaked until the next day?

不可以，因家裏調校的鹽水始終不及花蛤生活的大海，環境轉變了，花蛤容易死掉。
No. It is because salted water seasoned at home is not the same as the sea clams lived. They would die easily.

準備工夫 Preparation

- 花蛤洗淨，放入清水內，下鹽 1 湯匙浸 1 小時，取出。
- 粉絲浸軟；中芹切段；紅辣椒切圈。
- Rinse clams. Soak in water with 1 tbsp of salt for 1 hour. Drain.
- Soak vermicelli in water until soft. Section Chinese celery. Cut red chili into rings.

材料 Ingredients

花蛤 1 1/2 斤，乾粉絲 1 包（50 克），中芹 2 棵，紅辣椒 1 隻，蒜茸 1 湯匙，清雞湯 500 毫升，熱水 300 毫升
900 g clams, 1 pack dried vermicelli (50 g), 2 stalks Chinese celery, 1 red chili, 1 tbsp minced garlic, 500 ml chicken broth, 300 ml hot water

調味料 Seasoning

鹽適量
salt

做法 Method

1. 砂鍋內下適量油，加入紅辣椒及蒜茸爆香，放入花蛤煮片刻，注入清雞湯及熱水，加蓋。
2. 煮至花蛤的外殼剛張開（約 3 分鐘），加入粉絲及中芹煮滾片刻，下鹽調味，趁熱品嘗。

1. Put oil into a clay pot. Add red chili and minced garlic. Stir fry until fragrant. Put in clams and cook for a while. Pour in chicken broth and hot water. Cover the lid.
2. Cook for about 3 minutes until the shells of clams open. Add vermicelli and Chinese celery. Cook for a while and season with salt. Serve hot.

料理教室 CULINARY SKILLS LESSON

魚鮮 · 蝦甜 · 蟹香　SEAFOOD INDULGENCE

作者	Author
黃美鳳	Irene Wong
策劃/編輯	Project Editor
	Karen Kan
攝影	Photographer
	Derek Que
美術統籌	Art Direction & Design
	Ami
美術設計	Design
	Man
出版者	Publisher
	Forms Kitchen Publishing Co.,
	an imprint of Forms Publications (HK) Co. Ltd.
香港筲箕灣耀興道3號東滙廣場9樓	9/F., Eastern Central Plaza, 3 Yiu Hing Road,
	Shau Kei Wan, Hong Kong
電話	Tel: 2976 6570
傳真	Fax: 2597 4003
網址	Web Site: http://www.formspub.com
發行者	Distributor
香港聯合書刊物流有限公司	SUP Publishing Logistics (HK) Ltd.
香港新界大埔汀麗路36號	3/F., C&C Building, 36 Ting Lai Road,
中華商務印刷大廈3字樓	Tai Po, N.T., Hong Kong
電話	Tel: 2150 2100
傳真	Fax: 2407 3062
電郵	Email: info@suplogistics.com.hk
承印者	Printer
合群(中國)印刷包裝有限公司	Powerful (China) Printing & Packing Co., Ltd.
出版日期	Publishing Date
二〇一〇年七月第一次印刷	First print in July 2010

ISBN 978-988-19053-3-8
Published in Hong Kong

請貼郵票

寄

香港筲箕灣耀興道3號

東滙廣場9樓

「Forms Kitchen」收

Forms Kitchen Club

• 免費加入成為會員 •

• 尊享購物優惠 •

• 更多驚喜源源不絕 •

魚鮮·蝦甜·蟹香

歡迎加入 Forms Kitchen Club！

您的寶貴意見

為了出版更切合您要求的食譜，懇請給予我們寶貴意見，好讓我們更了解您的閱讀需求。

此書吸引您的原因是：(可選多於1項)

☐興趣　　　　☐內容豐富　　　☐封面吸引　　　☐工作或生活需要
☐作者因素　　☐價錢相宜　　　☐其他＿＿＿＿＿＿＿＿＿＿＿

您如何獲得此書？

☐書展　　　　☐報攤/便利店　　☐書店(請列明：＿＿＿＿＿＿)
☐朋友贈予　　☐購物贈品　　　☐其他＿＿＿＿＿＿＿

您覺得此書的書價：

☐偏高　　　　☐適中　　　　　☐因為喜歡，價錢不拘

您喜歡哪類食譜？(可選多於1項)

中式：

☐點心　　　　☐甜品　　　　☐飲品、湯　　　☐家常小菜　　☐粥粉麵飯
☐小食　　　　☐海鮮　　　　☐特色地方菜 (請列明：＿＿＿＿＿＿＿＿＿＿)

西式：

☐蛋糕、甜品　☐餅乾　　　　☐飲品　　　　☐批和撻　　　☐麵包
☐沙律　　　　☐燒烤　　　　☐扒類　　　　☐海鮮　　　　☐意粉
☐湯　　　　　☐你最喜愛的外國菜 (請列明：＿＿＿＿＿＿＿＿＿＿)

除食譜外，您喜歡閱讀哪類書籍？

☐玄學　　　　☐小說　　　　☐家庭教育　　　☐兒童文學　　☐語言學習
☐兒童圖書　　☐旅遊　　　　☐美容/纖體　　　☐現代文學　　☐消閒
☐商業創富　　☐其他＿＿＿＿＿＿＿＿＿＿

我們的小小心意

我們將會為您帶來最新的煮食情報及購物優惠！

*請填妥下列資料，剪出或影印此頁黏貼後寄回：香港筲箕灣耀興道3號東滙廣場9樓「Forms Kitchen Club」收，或傳真至：(852) 2597 4003，即可成為會員！

姓名：＿＿＿＿＿＿＿＿＿＿　☐男 / ☐女　　☐單身 / ☐已婚
職業：☐文職　　☐飲食業　　☐家庭主婦　　☐已退休　　☐其他＿＿＿＿＿
學歷：☐小學　　☐中學　　　☐大專或以上　☐其他＿＿＿＿＿＿＿＿＿＿
年齡：☐16歲或以下 ☐17-25歲　☐26-40歲　　☐41-55歲　　☐56歲或以上
聯絡電話：＿＿＿＿＿＿＿＿＿　電郵：＿＿＿＿＿＿＿＿＿＿＿＿＿
地址：＿＿＿＿＿＿＿＿＿＿＿＿＿＿＿＿＿＿＿＿＿＿＿＿＿＿＿＿＿

您是否有興趣參與作者烹飪分享活動？

☐有興趣　　　☐沒有興趣

您是否願意收到我們的最新書籍情報及各項優惠活動資訊？

☐願意　　　　☐不願意

*所有資料只供本公司參考